D1566010

DEPRESSION AS A PSYCHOANALYTIC PROBLEM

Paolo Azzone

University Press of America,® Inc.
Lanham · Boulder · New York · Toronto · Plymouth, UK

2-6-14
LN
$60.00

Copyright © 2013 by
University Press of America,® Inc.
4501 Forbes Boulevard
Suite 200
Lanham, Maryland 20706
UPA Acquisitions Department (301) 459-3366

10 Thornbury Road
Plymouth PL6 7PP
United Kingdom

Library of Congress Control Number: 2012950658
ISBN: 978-0-7618-6041-9 (clothbound : alk. paper)
eISBN: 978-0-7618-6042-6

In order to avoid any possible identification of patients alluded to
in the clinical material contained herein, all names of persons and
places as well as references to specific life circumstances have
been suitably altered.

Cover image by MILVIA

♾™ The paper used in this publication meets the minimum
requirements of American National Standard for Information
Sciences—Permanence of Paper for Printed Library Materials,
ANSI Z39.48-1992

Just like air, light, water, fire
whichever joy this worldly life
to me has spared,
Each leaf this shy and weary book does know
I owe to you,
Joan

TABLE OF CONTENTS

Prefatory Note

Freud was unsure whether or not psychoanalysis could offer a comprehensive understanding of *all* cases of depression. He believed that a somatic factor played a key role in the etiology of the illness, at least in "gewisse Formen der Affektion" ("certain forms of the illness," 1917, p. 440).

To some degree, Freud himself displayed a lack of confidence in his understanding of this point, and, over the last ninety years, an increased and still deeper lack of confidence has been detected among his followers. Together with dynamic psychotherapists operating within the field of psychiatry, they seem increasingly intimidated by the progressive advances in the neurosciences, all the more so given that these advances are accompanied by the expectation that biological psychiatry will benefit from them as will behaviorally, or symptom-oriented psychological treatments for depression. Nowadays, knowledge of the biology of depression is surely not lacking among medically trained psychoanalysts. They simply feel they must rely on it in order to offer a full explanation of the nature of depressive disorders.

My personal clinical experience, has, however, not been consistent with this. I frankly deem such a stance submissive. The longer I have been practicing dynamic psychiatry and psychotherapy (for over twenty years now), the more I have realized that an awareness of a patient's conscious and unconscious emotional processes can deeply illuminate the clinical phenomena that are being revealed to me.

I therefore felt the need to attempt to understand the roots of the overwhelming consensus I was confronting–in hospitals, in academia, in the media, and among patients, i.e. to understand this seemingly indissoluble link between depression and brain biology, an assumption which the majority of leaders in this field admit as unquestionable.

Social consensus is a social phenomenon (Moscovici, 2001). It can be understood only in cultural context and from a historical perspective. The first part of the book therefore introduces the reader to the long (more than bimilleniary) history of depression; its precursors in antique nosography are also discussed. The parallel between somatically based models of depression and physicians' social standing and social roles is emphasized and further competing explanatory models of prolonged mental suffering are also explored, i.e. Egyptian desert ascetics, ancient and Medieval philosophers and creative writers. Based on historical data as well as sociological analysis, I offer a possible explanation of the particular role that depression is currently playing in our society, a society in which medicine and associated sciences are expected to offer comprehensive answers to basic social questions.

In part II, I systematically investigate the symptoms of depression as they are conceptualized by descriptive psychopathology. Relying on Immanuel Kant's analysis of the knowing process, I show how a descriptive approach may inherently suggest that symptoms of depression are better conceptualized in terms of brain dysfunction. I then systematically demonstrate that a psychoanalytic understanding of depression can offer fruitful insights into any of its symptoms, outline the main contributions of psychoanalytic theory to the understanding of depression and discuss them in light of current psychiatric practice. My purpose in doing the latter is to demonstrate the immediate impact they can have on our understanding of this problem.

At this point, I hope the reader will agree, I am able to offer a comprehensive psychoanalytically based model for depressive psychopathology. I therefore show how *all* clinical phenomena of depression may potentially be conceptualized as psychic phenomena, *i.e.* in terms of an (unconscious) mind experiencing and processing painful events.

As for the questions at issue, we are unable to provide evidence to support the claim that the psychoanalytic understanding of depression is any more consistent with empirical data than other competing models.

However, we have been able though to show that the full spectrum of the phenomena related to clinical depression can *potentially* be interpreted in psychoanalytic terms. Now, after decades and after all of the research that is compiled in this work, we may be a bit more audacious than Freud, we do not *necessarily* need to assume the existence of a somatic factor: Depression can also be properly conceptualized as a psychic problem.

Acknowledgments

The author owes many thanks to Deborah Nash for her editorial job and for sharing so many comments and ideas about the text.

The Author gratefully acknowledges Guilford Press for permission to reprint the following previously published material: Paolo Azzone. "Looking through a distorted mirror: Toward a psychodynamic understanding of descriptive psychopathology of depression." *Journal of the American Academy of Psychoanalysis and Dynamic Psychiatry.* 2010, 38(4), pp. 575-605. Copyright © 2010 Guilford Press

Part I
Historical Facts:
Depression and Other Socially Shared
Representations of Pain in Western Civilization

Chapter One
Sadness and Black Bile

STABILITY IN CLINICAL DESCRIPTION

Since the appearance of the medical tradition in the Western world, sadness has been viewed as an illness, a somatic illness: " Ἢν φόβος ἢ δυσθυμίη πολὺν χρόνον διατελῇ, μελαγχολικὸν τὸ τοιοῦτον" ("If fear or sadness last a long time, this is a melancholic phenomenon")[1]. German E. Berrios (1995) and George Rousseau (2000) have stressed the differences existing between the clinical views of ancient melancholy and modern depression. However, the authors of Corpus Hippocraticum did not agree with moderns in that they did not grant to sadness a hierarchically superior diagnostic value with respect to psychotic symptoms that derive from fear (*cfr.* Galen, *De locis affectis*, III, X, ed. Kühn, pp. 189-190). They were nevertheless aware that that the clinical picture included poor appetite, abulia, sleeplessness, irritability, agitation ("ἀπόσιτος, ἄθυμος, ἄγρυπνος, ὀργίαι, δυσφορίαι." "Lack of appetite, aboulia, sleeplessness, irritability, agitation").[2]

Now, over 2400 years later, we are not only astonished by such an insightful clinical description. In fact, the Corpus Hippocraticum is rich in many other brilliant examples of extremely accurate, and substantially still suitable even today, clinical observations. It evidences extraordinary skill at grasping the essential elements of a syndrome without the help of modern statistics and a consistent knowledge of the etiology and pathogenesis of illnesses. The typhic state of *De internis affectionibus 39* or the nephritic state of *De internis affectionibus 14* are straightforward examples of this. But, what is truly striking is the fact that the Hippocratic description of melancholy has survived without any substantial changes or improvements having been made to it until the beginning of nineteenth century.

During the course of the centuries which distanced Hippocrates from Galen, the clinical picture acquired new details. The Roman encyclopaedist, Celso (first century A.D., *De medicina*), underscored some elements which differentiate melancholy from other diseases which have prominent behavioral symptoms: its outcome is more favorable than that of mania, and there is lack of fever typically associated with frenitis. Aretaeus of Cappadocia (likely to have lived in the first century A.D.), and later Rufus Ephesius (active at the beginning of the second century A.D.) documented the risk of suicidal behaviors and a number of characteristic delusional symptoms.

However, even 500 years after the writing of the *Aphorisms,* Galen does not essentially deviate from the Hippocratic writer: "Ὀρθῶς ἔοικεν ὁ Ἱπποκρατῆς εἰς δύο ταῦτα ἀναγαγεῖν τὰ συμπτώματα αὐτῶν πάντα, φόβος καὶ δυσθυμίαν" ("It appears that Hippocrates correctly referred all their [*scl.* of melancholics] symptoms to two: fear and sadness") [3] and like the Hippocratic writers, he thinks that black bile has a definite etiologic role: "ἅπαντες γοῦν ὀνομάζουσιν τὸ πάθος τοῦτο μελαγχολίαν, ἐνδεικνύμενοι διὰ τῆς προσηγορίας τὸν αἴτιον αὐτοῦ χυμόν" ("Everyone, then, calls this illness melancholia, showing through that definition the humour causing it") [4].

When the shadows of the darker centuries began to disperse from Europe and medicine began to re-establish itself in its traditional place within Western society, conceptualization and explanatory theories of melancholy did not change at all. Where melancholy is concerned, the medieval medical tradition drew on two main sources: Galen and Arabic medicine. The latter, while not lacking in original contributions, is largely dependent on Rufus Ephesius, whose treatise on melancholy, famous in antiquity, is now known only in excerpts. Still, these two traditions diverge minimally.

Ishaq Bin Imran, an Arab physician who flourished in tenth century, wrote an important treatise on melancholy. It became known in the West in the Latin adaptation by Constantinus Africanus. Following Rufus, Ishaq underscored the value of severe disorders of perception and of the content of thought in the clinical picture of melancholy but, in line with Hippocrates' *Aphorisms,* he stated: "Accidentia, quae inde fiunt animae, timor & tristitia videntur esse, quae utraque sunt pessima et anima confundentia" ("The symptoms which come from that to the soul seem to be fear and sadness, which are both very bad and confound the soul.") [5]

In essence, for the mediaeval physicians, melancholia remained an illness without fever, prolonged sadness and fear being its main symptoms. And, as we will later see more clearly, an excess of black bile was decidedly thought to contribute to its development.

The heavy conservatism of mediaeval culture can undoubtedly explain the persistence of diagnostic and etiopathogentic models of melancholy during the millennium that separated the fall of the Roman Empire from the discovery of America. However, the modern era also did not display a deeper capacity for investigation or innovation in this specific field of knowledge.

The sixteenth century has been defined the "Age of Melancholy." Richard Burton's work represents a sort of the summa of the knowledge of that age on this subject; it also demonstrates the extraordinary interest on the part of both the medical community and the society as a whole in this subject. And, yet, nothing had changed. Melancholy was still being described as "a kind of dotage without a fever, having for its ordinary companions fear and sadness without any apparent occasion." [6]

At the end of the age of enlightenment, thinking about melancholy began to change. It underwent a laborious transition. A host of classificatory endeavors interrupted the peace which had dominated the history of the disorder for two millennia. Melancholy came to be analyzed, distinguished from other diseases and classified anew. In the nineteenth century, the main criteria for differentiating functional psychoses appear to rest on the presence of, and be assessed in terms of, the extent of alterations to reality testing. Pinel (1801) held that melancholia was characterized by the circumscribed, focal quality of delirious manifestations, and his pupil Esquirol (1838) agreed with him. But Tuke (Bucknill and Tuke, 1858) did not deem reality testing a core factor, and acknowledged the existence of two forms of melancholy: simple and complicated, *i.e.* associated with delusional and hallucinatory symptoms.

Benjamin Rush (1827), the father of American psychiatry, stressed above all the focus of delusion, and suggested an original classification of affective disorders, based on two newly conceived nosological entities. In *tristimania*, which is basically analogous to traditional melancholy, the patient's ideation is focused on the Self, while in *amenomania*, which largely corresponded to the current concept of a manic episode, the subject is highly invested in the external world.

During the nineteenth century, medical theory underwent major changes. The improvements in medical semiology, the enormous advances in pathology, and the birth of clinical microbiology and of laboratory chemistry and physics all revolutionized the way in which knowledge of the human body and its diseases were organized. A new understanding of the etiology and pathogenesis of many disorders reshaped diagnostic and therapeutic resources and thoroughly affected the classification of illnesses.

Many clinical syndromes gave way to a differentiated array of distinct nosological entities. For instance, mechanisms controlling hydric equilibrium came to be largely understood and edema was now explainable in terms of organ pathophysiology in so far as it affected either the heart and circulation or the kidneys. Nothing like this was the case for melancholy, however. Throughout the century, many nososgraphical systems were proposed, but none of them could really be developed or expanded on the basis of the new knowledge of its causes and the mechanisms underlying the clinical syndrome, While von Krafft-Ebing (1879) suggested a pathogenetic classification of mental disorders, the scientific basis of this classification now appears to be clearly hypothetical.

Now that the twentieth century has come to the end, we can appreciate the fact that the nineteenth century nosography of melancholy left no significant trace in the subsequent century. The twentieth century construed depressive symptoms in a new and independent way, and the largely dominant perspective, one introduced by Emil Kraeplin, left a decided mark on the thinking of this century.

During the nineteenth century, psychiatrists tried to formulate rational criteria for identifying affective syndromes. Basically, they aimed to be internally
consistent with clinical descriptions. In the fifth and sixth editions of his treatise
(1896 and 1899), Kraepelin abandoned this approach, however. He worked
within the framework of the lunatic asylum, a modern and well organized structure. In line with the increasing capacity for handling the volume of information
available to the researcher in a modern industrial society, he relied upon precise
statistics on length of patient stays and recurrences of the illness. These were
essential to adequate planning for the ever increasing need for asylum beds and
services (Engstrom, 1995).

The management of an asylum required information analogous to that
which is more valued by the patient's relatives; above all, it needed to have a
reasonable capacity for foreseeing the progression of mental disorders. In this
connection, Kraepelin insightfully understood that affective psychoses are generally characterized by a *periodic* course, with a more or less complete inter-
episodic *restitutio ad integrum*. Into this category, the periodic psychoses cited
in the fifth edition of the treatise (1896), and the manic-depressive psychoses
discussed later (1899), he placed cross-sectional clinical syndromes commonly
called melancholia, mania and mixed states.

The clinical presentation of depressive forms is presented as follows.

> The *depressive forms* are characterized by psychomotor retardation, absence of
> spontaneous activity, dearth of ideas, dejected emotional attitude, prominent
> delusions and hallucinations, and usually clouding of consciousness. [7]

For Kraeplin, then, the content and intensity of delusional or hallucinatory experiences were less essential to the aim of characterizing manic depressive illness than was the alteration of mood. What mattered most was the speed of
cognitive and motor activity. Obviously, Kraepelin's description of depressive
forms of manic-depressive illness largely overlaps with clinical syndromes traditionally identified as cases of melancholia. As concerns cross-sectional symptomatology, Kraepelin's descriptions of depressive states are new only in terms
of the relative importance he gives to specific symptoms.

Kraepelin's most important contribution lies in a more precise appraisal of
the prognostic impact of affective symptoms in psychiatric syndromes in so far
as they are characterized by varying degrees of severity. This is precisely the
aspect of Kraepelin's thinking which survived him—the differing views and
particularly the theories by Eugen Bleuler notwithstanding—and which would
have an extensive impact on all of twentieth century psychiatry. After the great
Kraepelinian revival of the seventies, it would substantially inform DSM nosography.

While it has been officially adopted only within the United States, the Diagnostic and Statistical Manual of Mental Disorders (DSM), now in its third
and fourth editions (APA, 1980, 1987, 1994 & 2000a), is that nosographical
system which currently enjoys the highest reputation among psychiatrists

throughout the world, especially within the scientific literature. DSM disease classification includes a dichotomous conceptualization of psychoses, oriented on the opposite poles of schizophrenia and related psychoses on the one hand and, on the other hand, of affective psychoses. Kraepelin's approach is essentially accepted, even if some of its rigor is lost. The possibility that schizophrenia can be healed, albeit infrequently, is thereby acknowledged. Within the class of mood disorders, unipolar depression is kept distinct from bipolar disorders. The possible chronic course of mood disorders is stressed, and the prognostic view is more pessimistic than that expressed by the German psychiatrist.

We can now ask about the distance that separated the melancholy of Hippocrates, Rufus, and Galen and the Depressive and Bipolar Disorders of the DSMs. It is my feeling is that this distance is extremely short. Against the background of the extraordinary development of medical and general scientific knowledge, and particularly of medical statistics and epidemiology, semiology and, specifically, descriptive psychopathology, clinical description of depressive disorders progressed only by minute steps. Undoubtedly, the advances in psychopharmacology and Kraepelin's contribution gave our generation a better means of differentiating depressive disorders from delusional disorders. Nevertheless, most symptoms included in the DSM-IV list of diagnostic criteria for a Major Depressive Episode had already been mentioned in the *Aphorisms* of the Corpus Hippocraticum (depressed mood, sleeplessness, agitation, poor appetite and loss of interests: five symptoms out of the nine which are included in DSM-IV (APA, 2000a, p. 356). The possible occurrence of delusional phenomena had been extensively stressed since the period of Hellenistic-Roman medicine, as had the serious risk of suicide.

PREVAILING ETIOPATHOGENETIC THEORIES

Little, very little, has changed over 2400 years in the area of the nosography of depression. And, we now know very little more about its etiology or pathogenesis. As noted above, the author of the Hippocratic *Aphorisms* established a tie between prolonged sadness and other accompanying symptoms, and black bile. In a direct parallel to this, an excess of black bile was thought of as an essential feature of melancholic illness by most medical authors of Greco-Roman medicine, even though their main theoretical framework for the explanation of the pathogenesis of illness was not humoral, but rather eclectic (Rufus from Ephesus) or pneumatic (Aretaeus form Cappadocia). From the time Galen achieved his great synthesis and original reformulation of Hippocratic theory in the second century A.D., the concept of black bile not only played a predominant role in explaining the genesis of melancholy. In fact, it became an indisputably certain piece of knowledge for Byzantine medical theorists (Oribasius of Pergamon and Paul of Aegina, with the partial exception of Alexandrus of Tralle), in Arabic medicine (Ishaq Bin Imran and Avicenna), and then, through the translations by Constantinus Africanus and Gherardo da Cremona, in the Western medicine of the late Middle Ages. With the exclusion of the heterodox position of Paracelsus, this concept would remain the core factor in the study of melancholy throughout the sixteenth century. The treatises by André Du Laurens (1597) and Robert Burton (1628) attest to this.

Presently, humoral theory is taken to be an expression of a pre-scientific philosophy of medicine. The extraordinary success it obtained earlier was due to the fact that Galenic medical theory dominated Europe from late antiquity to the Renaissance. And, still the scientific status of etiopathogenetic theories of melancholy was not essentially changed through the course of sixteenth and seventeenth centuries.

Thomas Willis (1621-1675) was one medical theorist who openly opposed the humoral theory of melancholy: "... we cannot here yield to what some *Physicians* affirm that *Melancholy* doth arise from a *Melancholik* humor."[8] His iatro-chemical conceptualization of melancholy is, however, lacking any relation to the observation of patients or nature:

> ... let us suppose, that the liquor instilled into the Brain from the Blood (which filling all the Pores and passages of the Head, and its nervous Appendix, and watring them, is the Vehicle and bond of the Animal Spirits) hath degenerated from its mild, benign, and subtil nature, into an Acetous, and Corrosive, like to those liquors drawn out of Vinegar, Box and *Vitriol;* ... From the *Analogy* of these conditions, concerning the Animal Spirits, it comes to pass, that *Melancholick* persons are ever thoughtful, that they only comprehend a few things, and that they falsely raise, or institute their notions of them. [9]

Archibald Pitcain (1652-1713) was only able to formulate an hypothesis about the pathogenesis of melancholy. However, he had no doubt that a man could experience prolonged and deep emotional pain only if exclusively material events interfered with the usual functioning of his body (cfr. *Elements of Physick*, 1718, pp. 192-193). But, theories can change—and they did throughout the 1700s, and still more thoroughly during the 1800s and 1900s. The basic assumption behind them, however, did not: emotional suffering is an illness.

In the first decades of nineteenth century, psychiatry markedly stressed the moral causes of mental diseases and, in particular, of depressive states. For Pinel and Esquirol, the emotional factors traditionally associated to melancholy took on a great deal of weight, so much so that biological processes were nearly eclipsed in their explanations. However, their position implied an apparent rather than a substantial break with the previous psychiatric tradition. The next section more clearly describes how moral causes came to take on the role of factors negatively affecting the functioning of the brain. For Esquirol (*Des Maladies Mentales*, 1838, pp. 406-407), melancholy remained basically a "maladie cérébrale" the causes of which included an hereditary predisposition playing a very relevant etiological role.

However, the impact of the works by Pinel and Esquirol on the history of these theories of depression was limited. The extraordinary success of positivism and of the epistemology that flowed from it had a decided impact on the development of medicine. In the field of psychiatry, it led to the very rapid undoing of these provisional openings to the patient's emotional experiences. In 1845, Griesinger wrote the famous sentence: "Physiological and pathological facts show us that this organ [i.e. the one affected in mental disease] can only be the brain; we therefore primarily, and in all case of mental disease, recognize a morbid action of that organ" [10]. Kraepelin was operating within this conceptual framework when he constructed his nosographic model of manic-depressive psychoses and traced the origins of the illness back to a "neuropathic base." one which he took to have mainly genetically transmitted causes.

Melancholy, and subsequently depression, have represented and represent two models for conceptualizing mental pain in terms of signs of a bodily disease. Moral, and subsequently psychological, causes of depression have always played a secondary or marginal role in the history of psychiatry. In the next section of this work, we will attempt a more in depth examination of the description of these alternative hypotheses, follow their development from period of Greco-Roman medicine to the present day and then analyze the relationship between these conceptual models and those that have come to be dominant throughout history.

MORAL CAUSES OF MELANCHOLY

While the humoral model undoubtedly involved a perspective mainly focused on the body and bodily events, humoral medicine never denied completely the role played by emotional factors in the genesis of disease and particularly of melancholy. Rufus of Ephesus thought that an increase in black bile could be due, among other factors, to sadness and excessive concerns ("multa cogitatio et tristitia faciunt accidere melancholiam" [11], whereas Galen mentioned worry, moral suffering and sleeplessness as causes of melancholy, at least in those cases where other etiological hypotheses did not appear appropriate: "εἰ δ'ἐν εὐχύμοις ἐδέσμασιν [*scl.* ὁ ἄνθρωπος εἴη γεγενημένος], ἐπισκέπτεσθαι περὶ τε τῶν γυμνασίων αὐτοῦ καὶ λύπης καὶ ἀγρυπνίας καὶ φρροντίδος" ("If then [*scl.* the man has made use] of foods producing good humours, it is necessary to examine his physical activities, sadness, sleeplessness and worries" [12].

However, it was Arabic medicine, and particularly the treatise by Ishaq Bin Imran, which more clearly differentiated between the pathogenesis of melancholy, identified with an excess of black bile (and later with more or less hypothetical physio-pathological processes), and its etiology. It was from this point of view that the Arab physician distinguished congenital and acquired cases. In the latter, the increase of black bile could be due to a very wide array of factors, including the patient's life habits. A high degree of importance was assigned to these. Galen (*Ars medica*) had already identified factors of health and illness in life habits, and, in his works on the pulse, he had coined the term *non naturales*. But only in Byzantine and Arabic medicine did the expression *sex res non naturales* acquire its precise technical meaning, And, the great Bin Imran was the first ever to discuss in depth the impact of immoderate life habits on the possible development of a melancholic disease.

In Arabic and then Western mediaeval medicine the term *sex res non naturales* implied "six categories of factors that operatively determine health or disease, depending on the circumstances of their use or abuse, to which human beings are unavoidably exposed in the course of daily life"[13]. These are air, and generally the physical environment, exercise and rest, sleep and wakefulness, food and beverages, excretion and retention, and finally passions or perturbations of the soul.

From our point of view, of particular import is the role attributed to the passions:

> Quod autem dicendum est de eis, qui amata sua perdiderunt, sicut si filios & carissimos amicos amiserunt vel rem preciosam, quam restaurare non possunt, sicut sapientes libros suos subito amittentes, vel si cupidi & avari perdiderunt rem, quam non se recuperare sperent; haec omnia his gemitum & tristitiam & angustiam faciunt. Quae & mentes percutiunt & ad melancholiam paratas reddunt. [14]

> This, then, must be said of those who lost what they loved, such as their sons or their beloved friends, or a precious thing, which they can not replace, like scholars abruptly losing their books, or covetous or greedy men losing a thing they have no hope of getting back; all these things cause groans, sadness and anxiety to those people. These facts hit minds and make them ready to develop melancholia.

Among a number of dichotomies that marked the nosography of depression in the XX century, the distinction between depression reactive to life events and other forms of mood disorder (identified either as endogenous, or as neurotic cases) was met with a long-lasting consensus, especially among clinicians. Psychoanalysis tried to trace most cases of depression back to specific negative emotional experiences. Specifically, Freud (1917, p. 104) thought that "von mehr ideeller Natur" ("of a more ideal type") loss of a love object was the cause of many cases of depression.

Can the reflections by Ishaq Ibn Imran be analogous? By identifying in human passions and activities some of the causes of melancholy, did he break with the existing tradition? Did he explicitly hypothesize for the first time that the suffering which the melancholic patient incessantly laments is the representation of some real pain or affective experience?

Those pages in his work that are relevant to the problem of identifying etiological factors does not seem to warrant these conclusions. In Ishaq Ibn Imran's view, passions, like the other *res non naturales* are essentially factors which alter that equilibrium which exists inside the body:

> Haec enim [sex res] homini, dum vivit, necessaria sunt, cum de ipsis vel per ipsa sanitas sit vel imfirmitas. Quae si abundent plus, quam oporteat, mala in

corpore generatur materia. Unde corporis currumpuntur humores & corpus in hunc morbum [*sc.* melancholiam] labitur. [15]

In fact, these [six things] are necessary to man as long as he is alive, as from them or through them health or illness come. And if they are represented in a quantity that is higher than it is suited, a bad matter is generated in the body. And from that humours of the body are corrupted and the body falls in this illness [*scl.* melancholia].

Beef, pork, but also meat of goat, camel, boar and hare, are noxious as far as they generate a blood which is too dry or "turbidum & grossum." Cabbage, melon, honey, nuts, lentils, figs with nuts are so in so far as they "mutabilem sanguinem facientes & in coleram nigram redigentes." And, "multa quantitas suavitatis, quietis atque somni chymos colligit, qui post multa tempora mutati in choleram nigram sunt in causa istius morbi" [16]. In such a way, emotional reactions are not mirrored or represented in depression, but rather exhaust the physiological resources of the soul and so cause it to function poorly. In fact,

Sicut dixit Hippocrates in epidemiarum libris, sexta particula: Animae, inquit, labor est cogitatio. Sicut autem corporis labor pessimos generat morbos, utpote corporis labor, itidem & labor animae in melancholiam facit cadere. [17]

As Hippocrates said in his books on Epidemics, sixth section: Thinking is the labour of the soul. Then, as the labour of the body generated the worst illnesses, in a similar way, the labour of the soul makes it fall into melancholia.

From this perspective, the etiological role of the passions makes its way into the subsequent literature on melancholy as a factor which determines excesses of substances or exhausts the stamina of cognitive functions.

The study of the causes of melancholy will be met with great interest also over the ensuing centuries. To incorrect or immoderate life habits, to an abuse of the *res non naturales*, more and more factors are then added. In his famous treatise, Robert Burton mentions the following causes of melancholy: direct or indirect action of God or the devil (also through the intervention of magicians or witches), the influence of the stars, an hereditary predisposition, systemic or organ diseases, excessive or deficient exercise of sexuality, sour, thick, or thin beverages, black bread, unclean water, milk, oil, vinegar, fried food, shell-fish, head injuries, heat from the sun, or excessive sleep.

Besides this extensively abridged list of factors, we find in the etiological table proposed by Burton (*The Anatomy of Melancholy*, Synopsis of the First Partition), the passions or perturbations of the soul of the Galenic and Medieval traditions. In addition to sadness and fear, the passions implied by the melancholic disease, Burton's list includes shame, envy, hate, and those character traits that late antiquity and the Medieval traditions had conceptualized as mortal sins, i.e. drives or affective states which should be suppressed, as they were noxious to the health of the soul. From this point of view, Renaissance medicine is simply reflecting the idea that melancholy, or rather the excess in black bile through which melancholy finds a manifest expression, is due to a life style deemed inadequate, either inharmonious or insufficiently purified of elements which are deleterious to the Self, be they heavy food or lust.

As was true for the medical tradition that preceded Burton, the etiological table he developed includes an array of negative life events: financial upheaval, bereavement, various kinds of traumatic experiences and social problems. This section elicits our attention because negative life events play a major role in modern theories of the etiology of depression as well. Paykel et al. (1969) empirically showed that negative life events can enhance the risk of the onset of a depressive episode.

Can the inclusion of bereavement among what is a very wide range of possible causes of melancholy amount to the dawn of new insight? And can this reflect a still indefinite awareness that melancholy can indeed represent the manifestation of a painful experience? Do any ties exist between the conceptualization of bereavement as a cause of melancholy and the later Freudian hypothesis that melancholy is a manifestation of the affect felt in the soul in the case of the loss of a love object? Nothing allows us to think in this way. While from Arabic medicine to European Renaissance theories of the etiology and pathogenesis of melancholy become more and more elaborate, the basic assumptions underlying the conceptualization of the melancholic disease never actually changed. Very deep and long lasting psychic suffering is implicitly equated with a process of morbidity. While divergent affects or experiences can cause melancholy, this does not mean that it is either the representation of an emotional event, or a way of communicating the affect of some trauma or difficulty.

The very length of Burton's etiological list reminds us of the events that frequently depressed patients and their relatives mention when they are questioned about the reasons for their distress. The etiological theories we can observe in such circumstances are in fact equally various. The climate and its changes seem to have replaced the intervention of supernatural forces. But we find still bizarre neuro-physiological theories, various negative life events, including financial problems and various difficulties in work life, more or less significant instances of bereavement, marital conflict, misfortune in love and, above all, insufficient activity to be contributing causes–a list which closely parallels Burton's. Etiological theories of traditional medicine reveal an extraordinary parallel with the experience of sick people and their relatives, as far as we can observe it, in current clinical practice.

However, it can also be observed that, in humoral medicine as well as in that which is based on the more recent iatro-chemical and iatro-mechanical models, physical and psychical, biological and psychological causes can coexist, and no difficulty or intrinsic opposition between them has been perceived. Only at the beginning of XIX century did these poles begin to be perceived as opposing each other.

As we have noted above, with his *Traité médico-philosphique sur l'aliénation mentale ou la manie* (1801), somewhere between the eighteenth and nineteenth centuries, Philippe Pinel proposed an etiological theory of mental illness which gave unique weight to the moral causes of disease. According to Pinel, human passions are the "cause la plus ordinaire du bouleversement de nos facultés morales" [18]; and, he thinks he is warranted in stating that "dans le plus grand nombre de cas n'y a point de lésion organique du cerveau ni du crâne" (*ibidem*, p. 5).

However, his position needs to be accurately appraised. Drawing heavily on Crichton's (1798) reflections on human emotions, Pinel thought that emotions exercised their etiological action by interfering with the animal economy of the diseased. That is, they were deemed able to modify the mechanisms regulating the multiple functions which are essential for the survival and the health of our organism: the cardiovascular, respiratory, and neuro-vegetative systems, and the metabolism, but also memory, attention, impulse control, etc. The passage below makes it clear how Pinel thought *chagrin* affected the human being:

> Sentiment de langueur générale, chûte des force muscolaires, perte de l'appétite, petitesse du pouls, reserrament de las peau, pâleur de la face, froid des extrémités, diminution trés-sensible dans la force vital du coeur et des artéres, d'où vient un sentiment fictif de plénitude, une oppression, des anxiétés, une respiration laborieuse et lente, ce qui entraine les soupirs et les sanglots; ... sort d'ennui par les impressions répétées faites sur les organes des sens, éloignement extrême per le movement et l'exercice, qualquefois douleur vive dans l'estomac, circulation tres-affoiblie dans le vaisseaux du foie, ansi que dans les viscéres abdominaux; de-là marasme et un état de dépérissement lorsque le chagrin est tourné en habitude, c'est a-dire en mélancholie. [19]

> Feeling of general faintness, dropping of muscle strength, loss of appetite, smallness of pulse, stricture in the skin, paleness of the face, coldness in extremities, a very perceivable reduction of the living strength of the heart and arteries, which generates a fictitious feeling of plenitude, an oppression, some anxieties, and laborious and slow breathing, which causes sighs and sobbing; ... a sort of irritation with the repeated impressions on sensory organs, extreme aversion to movement and exercise, sometimes an acute pain in the stomach, a very faint circulation in the liver vessels, or in the abdominal viscera; from that marasmus and a state of emaciation, when sadness has become a habit, that is, has become melancholia.

Like the Greco-Roman and Arab physicians who preceded him, Pinel does not believe that melancholy can contain elements of truth or involve descriptions of real events. Rather, he thinks that emotions which are too intense break down the homeostasis of a mind-body system, thus causing errors in its functioning.

In essence, the etiological role of the passions in Pinel's thought should be understood in this restricted fashion. But, we must admit that, with him, and his pupil Esquirol, an opposition has been established between disorders due to the events of emotional life and those caused by biological factors lacking affective or relational meaning. In the course of the nineteenth century, however, most researchers' commitments will shift to the bodily pole. Such thinking is in line with the increasing success of positivistic epistemology. We mentioned above that, in 1845, Wilhelm Griesinger was able to state that "every mental disease proceeds from an affection of the brain."

The shift in student preferences continues throughout the remainder of this century and through the next one as well. It finds provisional appeasement in nosographical terms in the dichotomy between endogenous vs. reactive or psychogenic depression. The latter theory enjoyed a particularly wide acceptance in the middle segment of twentieth century. However, by this point it had become obvious that, over the last 30 years, the increasing consensus with which the biological paradigm has been met in the field of psychiatry has resulted in the institutionalized acceptance of a nosography largely based on Kraepelin's model, one in which the category of mood disorders plays a key role in the conceptualization and the hierarchical ranking of the disorders.

Depressive and bipolar disorders have constituted and still do constitute the preferred field for a model of psychiatry based on the identification of specific syndromes and symptoms, and on the use of drugs specifically devoted to their treatment. The breath-taking increase in the use of serotoninergic antidepressives and the extraordinary social success obtained by one of them (Kramer, 1993) make it clear that this approach has come to correspond with widely-shared social expectations of our time.

MELANCHOLIA AND THE BRAIN

Before we turn to discussion of sociological analyses, however, we must ask ourselves whether we can state that the hegemony of the biological paradigm in current conceptualization of depression can be connected to an increase in our knowledge of the biological bases of the higher functions of the human brain. If we look back to the origins of modern biological psychiatry and to its more famous representative between the nineteenth and twentieth centuries, the option to explain depression in biological terms does not appear to have been then based on empirical data. Kraepelin's opinions on the subject:

> Die Ursachen desselben [*scl.* des manisch-depressiven Irreseins] haben wir, wie es scheint, wesentlich in krankhafter Veranlagung zu suchen. Erbliche Belastung konnte ich in etwa 80% meiner Fälle nachweisen, vielfach gerade auch circuläres oder periodisches Irreseins bei anderen Familiemitgliedern. [...] [20]
>   Von sonstigen äusseren Anlassen ist die Entwicklung der Krankheit im allgemeinen unabhängig, ... Vielleicht der wichtigste Beweisgrund für diese Auffassung ist aber die Tatsache, dass die manisch-depressiven Geistesstörungen eine sehr ausgesprochene Neigung haben, im Leben mehrfach, ja sogar sehr häufig wiederzukehren; [...] (*ibidem*, p. 401)
>   Ueber das Wesen das manisch-depressiven Irreseins sind wir noch gänzlich im Unklaren . . . Wir können vorerst nur darauf verweisen, dass in unse-

rem Nervensysteme die Neigung zu periodischem Ablaufe der Hemmungs-
und Erregungs-Vorgänge auf den verschiedensten Gebieten wiederkehrt. (*ibidem*, p. 407)

We must look for its [*scl.* of manic-depresive psychoses] causes, as it appears,
essentially in a morbid disposition. I could recognize a family disposition in
about 80% of my cases, often directly represented by circular or periodic psychoses in other family members. [...]
    The development of the illness is generally independent of further exter-
nal causes, ... but perhaps the most important basis for this conclusion is the
fact that the manic depressive mental disorders have a quite manifest trend to
recur a number of times, even quite frequently, during the course of life; [...]
    About the essence of manic-depressive psychoses we are still completely
in the dark. ... We can for the time being only call attention on the fact that, in
our nervous system, there is a recurring tendency towards the periodic activation of processes of inhibition and excitation in the most diverse areas.

The observation that the melancholic disease aggregates in families dates back
as far as at least 450 years (*cfr.* Burton, 1628, Pt. 1, Sec. 2, mem. 1, Subs. 6),
yet family aggregation and genetic transmission are not identical. On the other
hand, the disposition to recurrent episodes of a mental disorder cannot be equated with biological causation as the etiopathogenesis and natural history of conversion disorder testifies (APA, 2000a, pp. 492-496.).

    And, although it still lacked a sound empirical basis, the biological option
remains very strong in the first half of last century and became still stronger after World War II with the discovery of psychopharmacology. In the 1980s, neo-
Kraepelinian thought triumphed.

    We are not obviously questioning the *current* results of scientific research
on depression. Nowadays, structural and functional techniques of neuro-
imaging, and immune-istochemicals and extremely refined knowledge of genet-
ics allow researchers to empirically answer to a number of questions relevant to
depressive illness. In this work, however, we wish to stress the fact that the assumption that the causes of depression are to be found in the body became con-
solidated at least 2400 years ago, i.e., well before empirical data could orient
students in this direction.

    Were the causes of depression looked for in the body and in the vital matter
constituting it in keeping with some sort of intuition? Or, due to the frequent
(but surely not constant) lack of stressful life events associated to the illness?
Before we try to answer to such questions, we must ask ourselves whether, in
modern medicine and psychiatry, any room is allowed for differing explanatory
paradigms which attempt to interpret depressive experience in terms of personality. We must ask whether and to what extent the Freudian psychoanalytic paradigm had an impact on medical sciences in their encounter with the depressive
illness.

    Eric Ehrenberg (1998 [1999], p. 169-170) observed that depression repre-
sented, at least quantitatively, a relatively marginal dimension of psychoanalytic

studies. Haynal (1977) stated that "... its importance does not seem to have always been acknowledged. It appears to have been overshadowed by the importance justifiably given to anxiety, with the result that in the relationship anxiety-depression the first of the two has been emphasized to the detriment of the other."

Freud's fundamental contribution to this subject is found in *Trauer und Melancholie* (1917). He there qualifies depression as an experience of pain. In his view, depression is differentiated from physiologically painful experiences like mourning the loss of a love object, by a) the narcissistic nature of the relationship to the object, b) the moral nature of the loss or c) the activation of massive defense mechanisms which can conceal in a more or less permanent and complete fashion the event which originated the experience of pain.

None of the phenomena which, according to Freud, characterize the experience of depression and differentiate it from other painful experiences seems to refer to biological, biochemical or bioelectrical events, and though he felt forced to assume the existence of "ein wahrscheinlich somatisches, psychogen nicht aufzuklärendes Moment" in order to explain given elements of the clinical picture and also asked himself whether "direkt toxische Verarmung an Ichlibido gewisse Formen der Affektion ergeben kann." ("a probable somatic moment, which could not be psychologically explained ... certain forms of the illness can result from direct toxic impoverishment of Ego libido." [21]

While Freud expressed some doubts that his model could allow him to exhaustively explain the genesis of all cases of melancholy, after World War II, psychoanalysts of the subsequent generations showed a limited and generally decreasing interest in depression as a specific syndrome of psychiatric nosography. Melanie Klein (1935) thought of the working through of depressive position as a key step in the achievement of a full emotional maturity, but the relationship between this internal object and defensive configuration and the depressive illness itself, although it was repeatedly emphasized by her, appeared substantially untenable to her pupils and followers (Hinshelwood, 1993 [1994], p. 82).

Actually, psychoanalysts who continued to operate within the neo-Kraepelinian framework of modern psychiatry adopted an extremely submissive attitude towards the prevailing biological theories. In the second edition of his work, *Psychodynamic Psychiatry* (1990), Glenn Gabbard, the main representative of this school of thought within North American psychiatry, which relies on psychoanalysis as an essential element of the theory of psychopathology, begins the chapter which is devoted to mood disorders as follows:

Affective disorders, like schizophrenia, are diseases with a heavy biologic component. Family transmission of mania and depression clearly indicates the core role played by genetic factors in the etiology. Neurochemical disorders are present too. ... unipolar depression is often alleviated when treated with triciclic antidepressant, with MAO Inhibitors, or electroshock treatment. The extraordinary research efforts of neuroscientists within the field of affective disorders raise the question whether there is actually a role, in these conditions, for the psycho-dynamically oriented psychiatrists.[22]

To this question Gabbard answered affirmatively, but the role of psychoanalytic therapies is thought of as an element which integrates and supports treatments based on different paradigms. In fact, a curious phenomenon takes place. Those who work outside the medical model of mental disorders and focus on the person do not seem to be particularly attracted by the study of, or the cure for, depression. On the other hand, depression is absolutely central among the interests of people who are looking at the mind in their search for the signs of a somatic illness.

The history of melancholy, from its origins to the present day, seems to lead us in the same direction. Since in Europe a lay, empirical, therapeutic practice, based on observation, *i.e.* a more or less rudimentary form of medicine, exists, there has been the belief that long-lasting pain is a form of illness.

The term illness is rich in differing meanings and defining it is not easy. According to Grmeck (1993, p. 323), the etymology of the different terms indicating illness in the various Indo-European languages "traces back to four thematic fields: a) weakness, lack of strength, loss of power in work, b) deformity, ugliness, c) uneasiness, malaise, and d) suffering, pain."

It is obvious that moral suffering, when it is deep and prolonged, is not entirely subjective since a more or less evident deficit in functions relevant to the family or social role can be observed in conjunction with it. From our point of view, however, it is essential to stress how tracing deep and long-lasting sadness back to an excess of black bile has some obvious implications: intense and prolonged suffering is undesirable; it is contrary to social expectations; it is the sign of incorrect functioning of the mind; it is not an adequate affective representation of the events in the personal life of the sick.

The validity of these implications could be discussed at length. Modern psychiatry has collected several elements which suggest a possible dysfunction in various neurotransmitter systems in cases of depressive illness (Green et al., 1995). Refined genetic studies would militate against the conclusion that the transmission of depressive illness is due entirely to environmental factors (Ries Merikangas & Kupfer, 1995, pp. 1108-1109). This is, however, not at issue here. Rather, we would prefer to underscore the fact that the status of the illness of melancholy was considered proven more than 2,000 years before empirical evidence emerged to support such an hypothesis. We would rather like to make clear that the development of medicine as a lay technology has been associated with the nosological conceptualization of melancholy.

Of course, we are not stating that melancholy either is or has been the product of physician observation; or, that it represents the projection on the symptoms, or more generally the person of the patient, of *a priori* categories of the physician. The contact with patients shows us everyday that some of the essential assumptions relied upon in the medical approach to the depressive illness correspond with great accuracy to the representation that patients give us of themselves. They frequently speak us about their condition of being an ill person as of being in a state of uncaused, or largely exaggerated, suffering; they talk about a dysfunction of their cognitive system, or the inability to control their own emotions. Depression takes shape then at the relational interface which becomes defined when a patient and a physician meet.

An Hippocratic text may perhaps help us to better illustrate the implicit assumption that a necessary tie exists between brain dysfunction and prolonged sadness. The *De morbo sacro* is a short polemic treatise included in the Corpus Hippocraticum. In this text the "μάγοι τε καὶ καθάρται καὶ ἀγύρται καὶ ἀλαζόνες" (*i.e.*, the healers operating within a magic-religious paradigm) are the object of ferocious criticism for their therapeutic activity towards people suffering from epilepsy. They claim to be professionals of the sacred. The attitudes expressed toward them are very hostile: a large room is allowed for gross devaluation of the opponents. Not only are their personal motivation often reduced to a mere longing for social and economic success, but the author strikes also us with his extreme inability to take into account the metaphoric value of religious theories of epilepsy and the possible suggestive effect of the proposed treatments.

Undoubtedly, knowledge from the modern field of neurology supports the conclusions of the author of this pamphlet: epilepsy is a disease of the brain. However, the high rate of functional crisis (as much as 30% of those admitted into the units for the monitoring of epilepsy, cfr. Pflaster & Pedley, 1996), which can occur also in subjects with a history of electroencephalographically documented crises, suggests that the interaction between mind and body is much more complex than has been heretofore supposed. And, this higher degree of complexity is, I believe, not acknowledged in the author's formulations when he presents us with a general theory of the human mind and of mental illness:

> Εἰδέναι δὲ χρῆ τοὺς ἀνθρώπους, ὅτι ἐξ οὐδενὸς ἡμῖν αἱ ἡδοναὶ γίνονται καὶ εὐφροσύναι καὶ γέλωτες καὶ παιδιαὶ ἢ ἐντεῦθεν [*scl.* ἐκ τοῦ ἐγκεφάλου], ὅθεν καὶ λῦπαι καὶ ἀνίαι καὶ δυσφροσύναι καὶ κλαυθμοί. [23]

> Men need to know that from nothing do pleasures and joys and laughter and jokes come to us than from there [*scl.* from the brain], where also sorrows, dejections, sadness, and weeping originate.

Here we find no place for personal history, processes of identification, interpersonal relationships, or the metaphoric use of language. The theory of mental illness that emerges from this point of view is univocal:

> τῷ δὲ αὐτῷ τούτῳ καὶ μαινόμεθα καὶ παραφρονέομεν, καὶ δείματα καὶ φόβοι παρίστανται ἡμῖν, τὰ μὲν νύκτωρ, τὰ δὲ καὶ μεθ' ἡμέρην, καὶ ἀγρυπνίαι καὶ πλάνοι ἄκαιροι, καὶ φροντίδες οὐχ ἱκνεύμεναι, καὶ ἀγνωσίαι τῶν καθεστώτων καὶ ἀηθίαι. καὶ ταῦτα πάσχομεν ἀπὸ τοῦ ἐγκεφάλου πάντα, ὅταν οὗτος μὴ ὑγιαίνῃ, ἀλλὰ θερμότερος τῆς φύσιος γένηται ἢ ψυ-

χρότερος ἢ ὑγρότερος ἢ ξηρότερος, ἤ τι ἄλλο πεπόνθῃ πάθος παρά τὴν φύσιν ὅ μὴ ἐώθει. [24]

Due to the same organ we get mad and our reason fails and terrors and fears are with us day and night, and also sleeplessness and inappropriate deceptions and worries which are not convenient and ignorance of the state of things and oblivion. And we suffer all these phenomena due to the brain, when it is not healthy, but has become more hot than usual, or more cold, or moister or drier or it undergoes some other affection differing from its usual nature.

I see a striking resemblance between this passage and Grisinger's statement. Two thousand three hundred years before positivistic psychiatry, the tie between depression or mental illness and brain damage was an accepted assumption. And, the author of *De morbo sacro* did not possess, as far as we know, any empirical evidence to support this thesis.

Curiously, his etiological theories are as fanciful as those argued for by the μάγοι who were his adversaries. *Exempli gratia*, with reference to mental pain: "ἀνιᾶται δὲ καὶ ἀσᾶται παρὰ καιρὸν ψυχομένου τοῦ ἐγκεφάλου καὶ συνισταμένου παρὰ τὸ ἔθος· τοῦτο δὲ ὑπὸ φλέγματος πάσχει." ("He feels pain and sorrow outside the appropriate occasion when the brain gets colder and more concentrated than usual. He suffers that due to the phlegm."[25]

The tie between depression and brain disease is not an empirical one, inferred from empirical observation. It is an *a priori* assumption which was met with extraordinary success for over 2000 years within the field of lay medicine.

DEPRESSION AND THE PHYSICIAN

Let us go back to the question formulated above: what structurally connects the theories and praxes of medicine to the biological model of depression? We can now introduce a first hypothesis. Lay medical practice happens whenever a professional stands by an ill man and concentrates on an array of elemental events relevant to his body. He takes notice of the color and temperature of the skin, of the rhythm of breathing, of the beating of the heart, of the quantity and quality of excretions and evacuations. He then analyses these elemental data in light of previous experience and locates information about these elemental events in the framework created by the past accumulation or transmission through the educational system of information about clinical syndromes. Finally, he acts on rational or empirical criteria with the aim of benefiting or healing the sick man.

The mental functioning of a lay physician is therefore characterized by a high control of emotions and of identification processes. Only in such a way can he focus on elementary phyiscal events without being overcome by anxiety about his fellow human being, who is suffering or at risk of death. Only in such a way can he gather and elaborate upon essential information and then apply procedures which can alleviate suffering or save life.

Let us now try to approach, with the same eyes, the same ears, the same fingertips, a man who is suffering in his mind, who has lost a loved one, a love, a source of gratification or interpersonal power. Now, we will be able to gather some elemental perceptions. We will be able to register the changes in the mimic, a reduction in the speed of movements, change in the physiological rhythms of sleep and hunger. The clinical picture of depression, or rather depression as a phenomenon, will take shape in front of our eyes. Once again, concentrating on the more elemental perceptions will allow us to take appropriate and important action in an easier way; to assess the risk of damage to the self, the need to be cared for or admitted to a hospital and to take note of indications and contraindications to drug therapy. The peculiar observational vertex or magnifying glass we have adopted is more suited to allow a rational working through of the events.

A similar style of information processing was described some time ago, generally at the first stage of human development, and, specifically, in the context of psychopathology. In his essential work, *Explorations in Autism*, Donald Meltzer (Meltzer et al., 1975) states that, in autistic states, the patient's self and his or her objects goes through a particular process of being disarticulated into their constituent parts. Meltzer called this "dismantling," and described it as follows:

> The 'dismantling' takes place through a passive device: letting the various senses, both particular and general, inside and outside, be attracted by the object that looks more stimulating at that moment. And it would be a mere coincidence if the most coloured sensations at the time, those whose shape attracts more the attention, the more odorous, noisy, tasteful, soft and hot will come all from the same real external object. With the exception of the newborn suckling the breast, such sensations are very likely to come at any moment by various objects; [26]

In essence, when dismantling is happening in interpersonal interactions, affective and ideational processes are not focused on human beings (man, woman, child, friend, enemy, servant, lord, physician, patient) but on elemental aspects of the object's body or mind: shape, colour or, within the medical framework, a patient's heart noises, electric fields, radiodensity.

While dismantling transforms and impoverishes experience by reducing it to its elemental components, the mechanisms of de-animation operate instead by changing the nature of the objects of the experience. The severely disordered child or adult who uses de-animation treats living human beings as physical objects. This obviously implies a basic attitude of indifference towards the emotional reactions that his behaviors can induce in others, their will and their sensations. Other people can be used, manipulated, moved, injured, controlled, all of that eliciting no guilt feelings or preoccupation with their fate. De-animation was defined by Margaret Mahler in 1968. According to her, it represents a defense mechanism typical in childhood psychoses.

Obviously, the defense mechanisms of dismantling and de-animation extensively overlap each other and commonly operate synergistically in order to transform experience. Both aim at sheltering the Self from emotions elicited by interactions with other human beings. In addition, the elemental parts of the experience of a human object, to which dismantling directs the attention of the subject, are much more suited to the action of de-animation than humans as a whole are perceived to be.

De-animation and dismantling have been described for the first time with reference to extremely early stages of development and to particularly severe psychiatric disorders. However, clinical research has progressively showed that these and analogous mechanisms can be observed, at least temporarily, in personality structures that are much more developed in terms of manifest functioning (Tustin, 1986).

In essence, the encounter with the emotionally suffering human being immediately elicits in the observer intense primitive defense mechanisms, aiming at defending his mind from the risk of a sudden and excessive identification with the sick. If the processes of de-animation and dismantling are happening, the resulting conceptual representation of the observed emotional processes will be depression.

At this point, however, we must stress that there are other ways of conceptualizing mental pain. We do not want to give the reader the impression (or delusion) that the terror of identifying with the suffering of our fellow human beings is a problem that is specific to either physicians or heavily medicalized societies. The experience of moral suffering has presumably created anxiety in any period of human history. Pain has been a constant object of concern by human cultures and by professionals who proposed to interpret it in social context and offered operative solutions to the different existential problems it poses. In antiquity and late antiquity, mental pain was also, and perhaps chiefly in terms of its social impact, the object of analysis using differing paradigms. In what follows, we will focus in particular on relevant philosophical and religious experiences, the prevailing paradigms for the conceptualization of emotional pain in Hellenistic-Roman culture and in late antiquity and the Mediaeval world.

NOTES

1. Hippocrates, *Aphorismorum Libri*, VI, XXIII.
2. Hippocrates, *Epidemiae, III*, 16 cases, case II.
3. *De locis Affectis*, III, X, ed. Kühn, p. 190.
4. Ibidem, p.191.
5. Constantinus Africanus, *De Melancholia*, B., p. 280.
6. Burton, 1628, 1,1,3,1.
7. Kraepelin, 1902, p. 283.
8. *Soul of Brutes*, 1683, p. 192.

9. Ibidem, pp. 189-190.
10. Quoted in Jackson, 1986, p. 163.
11. *Fragmenta*, p. 455.
12. *De Locis Affectis*, III, X, ed. Kuhn p. 184-85.
13. Rather, 1968.
14. Constantinus Africanus, *De melancholia*, B., p. 284.
15. Ibidem, p. 281.
16. Ibidem, p. 283.
17. Ibidem, p. 284.
18. Pinel, 1801, p. XXII.
19. Ibidem, pp. XXVII-XXVIII.
20. Kraepelin, 1899, p. 399.
21. Freud, 1917, p. 446.
22. Gabbard, 1990, p. 167, Ital. ed.
23. *De morbo sacro*, 17, 1-4.
24. Ibidem, 17, 9-18.
25. Ibidem, 15, 4.
26. 1975, p. 21, Ital. ed.

Chapter Two
Sadness, Error and Sin

SADNESS AND KNOWLEDGE OF HUMAN BOUNDARIES

In the later philosophy of the Hellenistic period, and then Roman imperial age, the movement most directly involved in the discussion of the experience of mental pain was Stoicism. A particularly widespread paradigm in modern psychotherapy, the cognitive paradigm (Montgomery, 1993), can be traced back to the Stoic ethic and anthropology, which is a source of its inspiration and provides models for identification. Beck (Beck and Weishear, 1989) recognized in Stoicism one of the sources of his approach to psychopathology. Ellis (1962) stated that "many of the principles incorporated in the theory of rational-emotive psychotherapy" were present in the thought of Epictetus.

On the other hand, the philosophical discipline which the Stoics termed ethics was not restricted to the identification of the principles of moral choice. The Stoic ethic constituted at one and the same time an educational path and an existential one. It that guided the individual in the development and transformation of personal identity. Moreover, it was a difficult path to tread, and required lengthy and demanding preparation and training. Stoic pedagogy has been described as a practice with essentially psychotherapeutic aims (Xenakis, 1969).

Moral pain was a point of particular interest to the Stoic. The Stoics did not conceptualize mental pain as an illness in medical sense. Instead, they aimed to outline an existential journey which was guided by reason. In the theory of the passions of Hellenistic Stoicism λύπη (sadness) was conceptualized as one of the four basic passions which could negatively influence the judgment of the subject and so move him away from virtue[1]. That is, sadness represented essentially a damnable and noxious giving way to emotionality.

While ancient medicine and Stoic philosophy agreed in representing suffering as a *per se* dysfunctional phenomenon, they also made reference to different explanatory paradigms and proposed differing therapeutic interventions. For

Hippocratic and, later, Galenic medicine, prolonged sadness expressed an unbalanced *crasis* of the melancholic humor; by contrast to this, the Stoics of imperial Rome took the phenomenon of mental pain to be the consequence of either cognitive error or inadequate information:

> Ταράσσει τούς ἀνθρώπους οὐ τὰ πράγματα, ἀλλὰ τὰ περὶ τῶν πραγμάτων δόγματα ˙ ... ὅταν οὖν ἐμποδιζώμεθα ἤ ταρασσώμεθα ἤ λυπώμεθα, μηδέποτε ἄλλον αἰτιώμεθα, αλλ'ἑαυτούς, τοῦτ'ἔστι τὰ ἑαυτῶν δόγματα. [2]

The man is not made upset by the facts, rather by his judgements about facts: ... therefore, when we are hindered or made upset or pained, we should blame no one other than ourselves, that is our judgement.

At the beginning of his *Manual,* Epictetus shows with extreme clarity the nature of such errors from his point of view. He distinguishes two types of objects of human aversion and drives: "τὰ μὲν ἐφ'ἡμῖν, τὰ δὲ οὔκ ἐφ'ἡμῖν... ἔργα" [3]. Love of objects who are under the power of others exposes us to an unavoidable burden of anxiety and pain.

Even though Epictetus is considered a representative of a moderate version of Stoicism, particularly with respect to the radical position held by the founder of the movement, Zeno of Cizio, his tolerance for the passions was very limited. Epictetus could not empathize even with the more spontaneous and natural emotions.

With reference to the experience of mourning the loss of a son, he writes as follows: "Μηδέποτε ἐπὶ μηδενὸς εἴπῃς ὅτι 'ἀπώλεσα αὐτό,' ἀλλ' ὅτι 'ἀπέδωκα.' το παίδιον ἀπέθανεν; ἀπεδόθη" ("Never say about anyone that you lost him, rather that you gave him back. Did your little son die? He was given back.").[4] And, he advocated taking a similar attitude of indifference toward the suffering of our fellow human beings:

> "Οταν κλαίοντα ἴδῃς τινὰ ἐν πένθει ἤ ἀποδημοῦντος τέκνου ἤ ἀπολωλεκότα τὰ ἑαυτοῦ, προσέχε μή σε ἡ φαντασία συναρπάσῃ ὡς ἐν κακοῖς ὄντος αὐτοῦ τοῖς ἐκτός, ἀλλ'εὐθὺς ἔστω πρόχειρον ὅτι "τοῦτον θλίβει οὐ τὸ συμβεβηκός (ἄλλον γὰρ οὐ θλίβει), ἀλλὰ τὸ δόγμα τὸ περὶ τούτου." μέχρι μεντοὶ λόγου μὴ ὄκνει συμπεριφέρεσθαι αὐτῷ, κἄν οὕτω τύχῃ, καὶ συνεπιστέναξαι· προσέχε μεντοὶ μὴ καὶ ἔσωθεν στενάξῃς. [5]

When you see someone crying in pain because a son is moving abroad or because he has lost his properties, be careful not to fall prey of the representation that he is victim of external adverse events, but have ready at your disposal the awareness that 'this man is not afflicted by what has happened (in fact, it does not afflict another), but rather by his judgment about it.' However, to the extent that it is a matter of words, do not hesitate to empathize with him, and, if it so happens, even to groan with him: but be careful not to groan inside.

THE SIN OF SADNESS

With the Stoicism of the Roman imperial age, the paradigm of illness gives way to that of error and guilt. The development and triumph of Christian religion brought Stoicism's social influence to an end, but as was repeatedly emphasized by scholars (e.g. Bonhöffer, 1911), the new religion, or at least its ethic, would nevertheless contain many parallels with this most eminent moral philosophy of the imperial age. From our point of view, it is particularly interesting to note that the Christian ascetic displays, since the period of earlier written documentation, an obvious hostility towards mental pain.

The Egyptian desert ascetic, like the stoic philosopher, aims at achieving control over his own passions. For Evagrius Ponticus, who systematizes and communicates, through the written medium, the experiences lived by generations of monks in the Egyptian desert, the endpoint of the ascetic path or πρακτική is ἀπάθεια, or impassibility. This was also the main goal of the path of personal development for the Stoic philosopher. The ultimate aims of each are undoubtedly different: for Evagrius, contemplation of the divine, for the Stoic, liberation from the conditioning of society and personal history. Also, the instruments and the means of realizing this path to perfection are similar: the Stoic's clarification of the errors of the mind gives way to or, rather, is supplemented by, the cognitive, affective exercise of the will, and the Christian ascetic works to free himself from the passions. The eight λογισμοὶ or δαίμονες, bad thoughts or demons that continuously threaten the impassability of the monk's heart, are essentially affects and drives: gluttony, lust, covetousness, sadness, anger, acedia, vainglory and pride. Among the serious dangers for the monk, two are explicitly related with the experience of pain: λύπη (sadness) and ἀκηδία (acedia), the latter term referring to a state of dejection, idleness, negligence and indolence. [6]

Tristitia

The tendency to condemn sadness persists from the Stoic theory of passions into the thought of the Evagrian ascetics without any evident break. However the reasons for mistrusting sadness did change. For Evagrius, it is not an *unfounded* feeling, lacking any apparent or intellectually identifiable basis. The sadness Evagrius treats is morally unacceptable because it is caused by the frustration of wishes: "Ἡ λύπη ... ἐπισυμβαίνει κατὰ στέρησιν τῶν ἐπιθυμιῶν" [7]. Although the wishes that torment the ascetic can be widely shared with reference to the ethics of laymen and religious men living within the general society, they are unacceptable for Evagrius as they tend to move the monk away from his sought after life condition:

Κατὰ στέρησιν δὲ τῶν ἐπιθυμιῶν οὕτως ἐπισυμβάινει· λογισμοὶ τινες προ-
λαβόντες εἰς μνήμην ἄγουσι τὴν ψυχὴν οἴκου τε καὶ γονέων καὶ τῆς
προτέρας διαγωγῆς. [8]

Owing to the frustration of wishes, the following takes place: certain bad
thoughts, presenting themselves, bring the mind to the memory of home, the
parents and the previous kind of life.

The condemnation of sadness, as elaborated within Eastern asceticism, was
handed down to Western Christianity through the works by Joannes Cassianus.
In his *De coenobiorum institutis* written at the request of Castor, bishop of the
now French town of Apt, in the first half of the fourth century A.D., Cassianus
presents to Western monks the principles that regulate the religious life of their
Egyptian brothers. The ascetic experience of the latter constituted a long standing tradition and was highly respected.

Cassianus made extensive use of the ascetic works of Evagrius Ponticus
and drew from him the list of the eight bad thoughts. But he, too, warned
against the danger of sadness and, like Evagrius, traced its roots back to the
frustration of worldly wishes. Drawing on a point of view not so remote from
that of Roman Stoicism, Cassianus concluded that indifference towards material
goods was the only path to freedom from pain:

> Hanc ergo perniciosissimam passionem ita de nobis expellere poterimus ut
> mentem nostram spiritali meditatione jugiter occupatam futura spe et contem-
> platione repromissae beatitudinis erigamus ... cum aeternarum rerum ac fu-
> turarum intuitu semper laeti, atque immobiles perdurantes, nec casibus dejecti
> presentibus, nec prosperis fuerimus elati, utraque velut caduca et mox transe-
> untia contemplantes. [9]

> We will be able to expel from ourselves this very harmful passion only as far
> as we are able to uplift our minds, so that, through spiritual meditation, it is
> continuously engaged with the future hope and the contemplation of the prom-
> ised happiness. ... always happy because of the vision of the eternal and future
> things, and unwaveringly persisting, we will be neither dejected by current ad-
> versities, nor elated by current lucky events, viewing both as of short duration
> and transient.

The Western Cassianus proposed a more finely-tuned understanding of the experience of sadness than the one presented in Evagrius's πρακτική. According
to Cassianus, two forms of sadness can be differentiated: the sadness that leads
to repentance and worldly sadness. The two are distinguished by their different
origins, but, above all, by their different spiritual sequelae. The sadness that
comes from the awareness of sin "obediens est, affabilis, humilis, mansueta,
suavis et patiens, utpote ex Dei charitate descendens" [10]. On the other hand, the

sadness implying the frustration of a wish is "asperrima, impatiens, dura, plena rancore et moerore infructuoso, ac desperatione poenali, eum quem complexa fuerit ab industria ac salutari dolore frangens ac revocans" [11]. The Pauline sources of this differentiation will be discussed in greater detail later in this chapter.

Acedia

As mentioned, besides sadness, Evagrius took into account a second bad thought which overlaps closely with the experience of emotional pain: *acedia*. Contrary to sadness, *acedia* had been substantially ignored by the preceding philosophical tradition. It would, however, come to enjoy extraordinary success as a theory in the course of the next thousand years. In classical Greek, *acedia* means "neglect, indifference." In the translation of the Bible produced by the Seventy, it has the meaning of discouragement. Although the term had been sporadically present in anchoretic literature,[12] there is no doubt that it was Evagrius who introduced it as one of the main vices identified in the monastic literature of both East and West.

Since late antiquity, *acedia* has been construed as a mental state very near to sadness. Over the centuries, it came to be thought of as synonomous with sadness. As early as the fourth century A.D., Gregorius Magnus considered both of these to be expressions of an essentially unitary emotional state and referred to them with the common term of *tristitia*.[13] Since that point, experiences of pain-discouragement-dejection, and weak commitment or sloth in the practice of religion were viewed in essentially the same way by ascetics as well as moralists and theologians. The terms *acedia* and *tristitia* came to be interchangeable.

Actually, in the work of Evagrius Ponticus, the two subjective experiences of sadness and of acedia appear to be clearly distinguished. In his description of λύπη, Evagrius did not essentially move away from the preceding and subsequent traditions; ἀκηδία, on the other hand, does not seem to be simply synonymous with inertia or inactivity in religious matters. The following excerpt makes this clear:

Καὶ πρῶτον μὲν τὸν ἥλιον καθορᾶσθαι ποιεῖ δυσκίνητον ἢ ἀκίνητον, πεντηκοντάωρον τὴν ἡμέραν δεικνύς. Ἔπειτα δὲ συνεχῶς ἀφορᾶν πρὸς τὰς θυρίδας καὶ τῆς κέλλης ἐκπηδᾶν ἐκβιάζεται, τῷ τε ἡλίῳ ἐνατενίζειν πόσον τῆς ἐνάτης ἀφέστηκε, καὶ περιβλέπεσθαι τῇδε κἀκεῖσε μή τις τῶν ἀδελφῶν. Ἔτι δὲ μῖσος πρὸς τὸν τόπον ἐμβάλλει καὶ πρὸς τὸν βίον αὐτόν, καὶ πρὸς τὸ ἔργον τὸ τῶν χειρῶν· καὶ ὅτι ἐκλέλοιπε παρὰ τοῖς ἀδελφοῖς ἡ ἀγάπη καὶ οὐκ ἔστιν ὁ παρακαλῶν· εἰ δὲ καί τις κατ᾽ ἐκείνας τὰς ἡμέρας εἴη λυπήσας τὸν μοναχόν, καὶ τοῦτο εἰς αὔξησιν τοῦ μίσους ὁ δαίμων προστίθησιν. Ἄγει δὲ αὐτὸν καὶ εἰς ἐπιθυμίαν τόπων ἑτέρων ἐν οἷς ῥᾳδίως τὰ πρὸς τὴν χρείαν ἔστιν εὑρεῖν καὶ τέχνην μετελθεῖν εὐκοπώτεραν μᾶλλον καὶ προχωροῦσαν... [14]

And at first it makes the sun appear as though it is moving slowly or not at all, as if the day is lasting 50 hours. Afterwards, it compels [the monk] to continuously peer out of the shutters, and walk out of the cell, in order to assess the position of the sun and measure how long it will take to reach the ninth hour, and to look around in case one of the brothers may be arriving. In addition, it elicits a hatred for the place, and even for monastic life, and for manual work: adding that the brothers' love has abandoned [the monk] and that there is no one comforting him: and if someone has also hurt the monk in those days, the demon brings this forth, too, in order to enhance the hatred. And, it leads him to the wish for removal to other places in which it would be easier to find what is needed and to follow a more comfortable and prosperous craft.

The devil of *acedia* approaches the monk at a specific time of the day ("...ἐφίσταται μὲν τῷ μοναχῷ περὶ ὥραν τετάρτην, κυκλοῖ δὲ τὴν ψυχὴν αὐτοῦ μέχρις ὥρας ὀγδόης," "It approaches the monk about the fourth hour, and is up to his soul till the eighth hour") [15]. It is more specifically characterized by anxious expectation for the presence of other anchorite brothers.[16] To this waiting, and implicit wish, were attached feelings of rancor towards those brothers who were absent and phantasies about immediate wish satisfaction in terms of reduced physical labor and more material rewards.

The phantasy dominating the anchorite, who falls prey to acedia, seems to allude to the wish to meet those human beings with whom he shares his life and to refer to the obvious experience of frustration enforced by the rigid rules of the coenobium. The latter allowed the monk to experience interpersonal relationships only within very restricted temporal boundaries (essentially only at the evening meals or on feast days). From such experiences of frustration phantasies did develop. They were based on projective identification phenomena[17] within which the experience of frustration and the dependency became inverted and the community of brothers suffered from abandonment and rejection by this ascetic who would depart for new lands.

We can only speculate about how very essential Evagrius's meeting with his brothers was – and this on the basis of the remedies he proposed to the evil of acedia. Evagrius is generally very harsh towards himself, his own body and his own passions. To those unable to sustain the very rigid dietary regimen of the Anchorites, he suggests: reduce bread and even water ("Ὁπηνίκα διαφόρων βρωμάτων ἐφίεται ἡμῶν ἡ ψυχή, τὸ τηνικαῦτα ἐν ἄρτῳ στενούσθω καὶ ὕδατι" [18]. The compassion he can demonstrate toward the soul laboring under acedia is therefore all the more surprising:

Ὅταν τῷ τῆς ἀκηδίας περιπέσωμεν δαίμονι, τὸ τηνικαῦτα τὴν ψυχὴν μετὰ δακρύων μερίσαντες τὴν μὲν παρακαλοῦσαν τὴν δὲ παρακαλουμένην ποιήσωμεν, ἐλπίδας ἀγαθὰς ἑαυτοῖς ὑποσπείροντες καί τό τοῦ ἁγίου Δαυῒδ κατεπᾴδοντες· ἵνα τί περίλυπος εἶ, ἡ ψυχή μου, καὶ ἵνα τί συνταράσσεις με; ἔλπισον ἐπὶ τὸν Θεόν, ὅτι ἐξομολογήσομαι αὐτῷ· σωτήριον τοῦ προσώπου μου καὶ ὁ Θεὸς μου. [19]

Whenever we give in to the demon of acedia, then splitting the soul with tears let us make it into two parts, the first one comforting, the second one comforted, diffusing good hopes for ourselves and singing the words by saint David: 'Why are you sad, my soul, and why do you upset me? Hope in God, because I will attest to him: saviour of my face and my God.

The sweetness and attentiveness that characterizes the remedy proposed for acedia stand in sharp contrast to the strict attitude, perhaps even imbued with perceptible tinge of sadism, that Evagrius displayed when he was confronted with other devils. We clearly feel the presence of a maternal, caring attitude overlapping closely with those maternal cares which, in Winnicott's view (1953), are at the core of both the human development and psychoanalytic process.

Both Cassianus [20], and Evagrius [21] supplement their descriptions of the vice of *acedia* by narrating an autobiographic episode. In both cases, our ascetics seek the help of a master who was older or somehow more experienced in resisting the devil of acedia. Cassianus specifies that it was precisely to this end that he had left his cell, during a savage attack of this malicious spirit. He did so under the pressure of a desperate wish to meet a human being, to gratify his wishes for contact and dependence. But his request met with no acceptance: rather the experienced ascetic blamed him and urged him to stay in his own cell. Neither did Evagrius, who, incidentally, did not specify at which time he had expressed his request for help – indicate a greater willingness:

Ἔλεγε δὲ ὁ ἅγιος καὶ πρακτικώτατος ἡμῶν διδάσκαλος· οὕτω δεῖ ἀεὶ παρασκευάζεσθαι τὸν μοναχὸν ὡς αὔριον τεθνηξόμενον, καὶ οὕτω πάλιν τῷ σώματι κεχρῆσθαι ὡς ἐν πολλοῖς ἔτεσι συζησόμενον. Τὸ μὲν γάρ, φησί, τοὺς τῆς ἀκηδίας λογισμοὺς περικόπτει καὶ σπουδαιότερον παρασκευάζει τὸν μοναχόν· τὸ δὲ σῶον διαφυλάττει τὸ σῶμα καὶ ἴσην αὐτοῦ ἀεὶ συντηρεῖ τὴν ἐγκράτειαν. [22]

And our master, saint and experienced with the ascetic life, used to say: the monk need always to prepare himself as if he was to die the morrow, but on the other hand to so use his body as though he should survive for many years. In fact, the former attitude—he said—hinders the bad thought of acedia and prepares the monk to be more ready: the latter safeguards the body and keeps it constant in abstinence.

The piece of advice Evagrius received appears frankly moralistic and trivial, but it again stresses the intensity of the anxiety connected with the time, i.e. with the expectation of the relating to the object. The solitary ascetic in his afternoon hours is inwardly divided between the longing to get in touch with the brothers he loves and the experience–likely to be customary if we have to assign exemplary value to the concrete episode referred by Cassianus–that outside of the predefined limits, his brothers are not available to him. From this point of view, then, the devil of acedia alludes to separation anxieties as they can be perceived in a setting which very rigidly regulates the experiences of interpersonal contact, and among subjects for whom the forces blocking interpersonal relations can easily prevail against efforts to establish a more intense contact. In fact, Cassianus himself was aware that acedia is "vagis maxime ac solitariis magis experta" [23]

However, this aside, relative to the need for interpersonal contact, Evagrian acedia obviously has another feature: difficulty in concentrating on prayer and work; also, inertia often gives way to sleepiness. This feature may be less evident in the discussion of acedia of Evagrius as it is included in the Πρακτική. On the other hand, in the *De octo spiritibus malitiae*, Evagrius more sharply underscores this dimension, more in line with the core etymology of the word acedia:

> Ἀναγινώσκων ἀκηδιαστὴς χασμᾶται πολλά, καὶ πρὸς ὕπνον καταφέρεται εὐχερῶς, τρίβει τὰς ὄψεις, καὶ διατείνει τὰς χεῖρας, καὶ τοῦ βιβλίου τοὺς ὀφθαλμοὺς ἀποστήσας, ἐνατενίζει τῷ τοίχῳ, πάλιν ἐπιστρέψας ἀνέγνω μικρὸν, καὶ ἀνάπτυσσων τὰ τέλη τῶν λόγων περιεργάζεται, ἀριθμεῖ τὰ φύλλα, καὶ τὰς τετράδας ἐπιψηφίζει, ψέγει τὸ γράμμα καὶ τὴν κόσμησιν, ὕστερον δὲ πτύξας ὑπέθηκε τῇ κεφαλῇ τὸ βιβλίον, καὶ καθεύδει ὕπνον οὐ πάνυ βαθύν, ἡ γὰρ πεῖνα λοιπὸν διεγείρει αὐτοῦ τὴν ψυχήν, καὶ τὰς ἑαυτῆς φροντίσεις ποιεῖ. [24]

> When reading, the man troubled by acedia yawns a lot, and easily falls asleep, rubs his face, and extends his hands, and, moving the eyes away from the book, examines the wall, turning back again, he reads a little, and wastes his time turning over the pages in order to see where the text ends, counts the leaves, and calculates the number of the quaternions, finds fault with the handwriting and the ornamentation, finally, having closed the book, puts his head on it and sleeps quite a superficial sleep, in fact then the hunger awakes his soul, and he takes care of his business.

For his part, Cassianus insisted that the intolerance for the cell is associated with a slowing and blurring of mental processes:

> ... et ita quadam irrationabili mentis confusione, velut tetra suppletur caligine, omnique actu spiritali redditur otiusus ac vacuus, ut nulla re alia tantae oppugnationis remedium, quam visitatione fratris cujuspiam, seu somni solius solatio posse aestimet inveniri. [25]

and so, owing to a certain irrational confusion of mind, it is filled by a dark fog, and becomes idle and empty of any spiritual action, so that he thinks that in no other thing can be found a remedy for such an opposition, than in visiting some brother or in the restoration of sleep.

We may now ask ourselves which rapport ties restlessness and intolerance for the loneliness of the cell with the low productivity and the difficulty in concentrating. The blurring of mental processes Cassianus is talking about can, in our view, be interpreted in light of the original theory of thought processes developed by Wilfred R. Bion (1962). The phenomenon described by Cassianus can then be conceptualized as the effect of an excess of ß elements, *id est* of emotion or precursors of emotions which saturate the subject's cognitive and affective processing potential.

The suffering and helplessness content of ß elements comes to be expressed through a feeling of fatigue or creative inhibition, while manic defenses that are activated in order to contain the excess of pressure on the mind find phenomenic manifestation in the effort at evading the experience of frustration through action (getting out from the cell, seeking to be listened to by an older monk). Acedia, then, in Evagrius's and Cassianus's thought, seem to allude to experiences in which the mental apparatus becomes overburdened. It is then associated with the effort at finding emotional containment and nurturance in the interpersonal encounter. Acedia phenomenologically evidences the difficulties which hinder the satisfaction of these needs within the rigid limits that regulate interpersonal relationships in monastic communities.

ACEDIA AS IT OCCURS OUTSIDE MONASTIC WALLS.

Acedia and Productivity

When the concept of acedia, and more generally the reflection on capital vices came to be understood in a more widely diffused manner and extended beyond the limits of the monastery, particularly in western Christendom, it tended to lose the features which correlated it specifically to the experience of monastic life. In the works of Cassianus, it had already undergone a semantic extension and come to indicate more of a character trait than a state of mind or soul, something above and beyond fatigue and somnolence. It was now understood as including low productivity and effectiveness. The latter had initially been construed as a lack of motivation and eventually came to overlap conceptually with sloth. It is of laziness or sloth that Cassianus is thinking when he proposes an extended exegesis of the second letter of Saint Paul to the Thessalonians in the context of his discussion of the spirit of acedia.

St. Paul there stigmatizes the attitude of those within the Christian community of Thessaloniki who adopted a socially dependent and rowdy lifestyle and refused to dedicate themselves to productive work (*cfr.* 2 Thess 3: 6-13). These life choices, perhaps dictated by spiritual motivations, made him very fearful. He is likely to have been afraid that millenarianistic expectations would endanger the integration of the Christian community into the larger social and productive social body, and so, in the long run, make its survival impossible within pagan society. Whatever the case may have been, Cassianus seems to agree with the Pauline point of view and to share the intense anxiety that low levels of productivity can corrupt the entire social body:

> Itaque ab his qui vacare operi nolunt, jubet subtrahi, et velut membra otii corrupta putredine desecari; ne inertiae morbus, velut lethale contagium, etiam sanas membrorum partes tabe serpente corrumpat. [26]

> So it is necessary to withdraw from those who do not want to work, and cut them away as limbs corrupted by the rottenness of idleness; so that the illness of idleness, like a fatal form of contagion does not also corrupt healthy limbs when the sickness is diffused.

At any rate, in the first letter to the Thessalonians Paul had underscored the ethical value of work: "νυκτὸς καὶ ἡμέρας ἐργαζόμενοι πρὸς τὸ μὴ ἐπιβαρῆσαί τινα ὑμῶν ἐκηρύξαμεν εἰς ὑμᾶς τό εὐαγγέλιον τοῦ θεοῦ." [27] And, the author of the second letter to Thessalonians expressed himself even more harshly: "καὶ γὰρ ὅτε ἦμεν πρὸς ὑμᾶς, τοῦτο παρηγγέλλομεν ὑμῖν, ὅτι εἴ τις οὐ θέλει ἐργάζεσθαι μηδὲ ἐσθιέτω." [28]

As we have seen, Paul and the author of the second letter to Thessalonians are chiefly worried with the relationship between a socially dependent life style and moral disorder, a behavior which the Letter defined as ἀτάκτως περιπατεῖν (2 Thess. 3: 6), i.e. living in an unordered way. Cassianus adopted the same point of view:

> Mens enim otiosi nihil aliud cogitare novit, quam de escis ac ventre, donec inventa quandoque sodalitate cujusqam viri, vel feminae aequali tepore torpentis, rebus eorum ac necessitatibus involvatur; et ita paulatim reddatur noxiis occupationibus irretitus, ut tamquam serpentinis spiris obstrictus numquam deinceps ad perfectionem professionis antiquae se valeat enodare.[29]

> In fact the idle man's mind can think of nothing other than of foods and the bowel, as long as, having found at a certain time the company of any man or woman who is paralyzed due to the same lack of energy, he gets involved in their affairs and attends to their needs; and, so, little by little, he is imprisoned in noxious occupations. Thus, held tightly, so to speak, by snake coils, he is never again able to free himself and come back to the perfection of his old way of life.

With Cassianus, then, acedia acquired a new dimension. In the East, the passion of acedia had involved designating a specific difficulty which a monk was having in concentrating on the ascetic and mystical experience. When it reached the West, the concept of acedia came to include in its semantic horizon the more trivial and lay phenomenon of the love for rest. In other words, it had shifted from meaning a difficulty in concentrating to meaning a deficit of the will, the latter, frankly, overlapping with sloth and so bordering on social parasitism.

The reliance on the ethical value of labor has been one of the core features of western Christendom from the time of Benedictus of Norcia to Calvin; it later imbued the lay values of bourgeois society with meaning (Weber, 1905). With Cassianus, the hostility towards dependence and parasitism are incorporated into the monastic value system. The discussion of acedia is the path through which he effected this shift.

For monks and Christians, reflection on negative passions persisted through the centuries of mediaeval Christendom. But the prevailing form, and later the only one, adopted by such reflection is not the list of eight vices developed by Evagrius and Cassianus, but rather the list of seven developed by Gregorius Magnus.[30] As mentioned, in his lengthy meditation on the book of Job, Gregorius reformulated and simplified Evagrius's system. The two vices associated with the experience of mental pain (λύπη and ἀκηδία), then came to be grouped under the common name of *tristitia*.

From this point onward, Christian ethics would condemn, either under the name of tristitia, or under the name of acedia, three well defined classes of emotional experiences: a) states of depression and desperation, b) inertia, drowsiness, psychomotor slowing, and c) laziness, low levels of activity in the domain of the spiritual, but also the mundane.[31] The relative weight assigned to each of these three aspects of the vice, referred to as *acedia vel tristitia* in the Middle Ages by Petrus Lombardus as well as by Hugo de Sancto Victore, varied widely according to several social factors. And, this was the case until the increasing prevalence of the mundane component in the centuries leading from the Middle Ages to the Renaissance.

The Conceptualization of Acedia in Mediaeval Lay Literature

There is extensive evidence of such evolution in the lay literature of the last centuries of the Middle Ages, a literature which is marked by a deep interest in the configuration of the human personality and its distortions. Numerous literary texts from this period treating of the virtues and vices discuss the sin of *acedia vel tristitia*. We here review three prominent examples.

Sadness: A Handicap for Courtly Lovers

The first part of the *Roman de la rose*, written around 1230 by Guillaume de Lorris, expresses in the form of a refined allegory the values and erotic ideals of the French aristocracy at the beginning of the XIII century. At the time, the society was still dominated by the paradigm of courtly love. In order to gain access to the garden of *Deduit*, where love rituals are celebrated, the main character in this first part of the romance must go through a wall. On that wall were represented all of the bad inclinations and lifestyles which were deemed incompatible with the loving life as conceived by the aristocracy.

The vice of *acedia vel tristitia* is represented under the heading of *Tristece*. Guillaume's description particularly stresses depression of mood and reduction in appetite and weight loss, as well as lack of interest and ability to react to positive stimulation.

> Delez anvie auques pres iere
> Tristece pointe en la mesiere.
> Mes bien paroit a sa color
> Qu'el avoit au cuer grant dolor
> El sambloit avoir la jaunice,
> Si n'i feïst riens avarice
> De paleté ne de megrece,
> Car li esmais et la tristece
> Et la pesance et li anuiz
> Qu'el soffroit de jor et de nuiz,
> L'avoient faite mout jaunir
> Et maigre et pale devenir.
> Onques riens nee a tel martire
> Ne fu mes ne n'ot si grant ire
> Com il sembloit qu'ele eüst.
> Je cuit que nus ne li seüst
> Faire rien que li poïst plaire
> Ne ne se vousist pas retraire
> Ne reconforter a nul fuer
> Dou duel qu'ele avoit a son cuer [32]

Beside envy to some distance painted/ sadness was on the wall./ But it well appeared because of its colour/ that it had a great pain at its heart./ It seemed to have jaundice,/ and you would value nothing covetousness/ in terms of paleness and slimness,/ because the worries and the sadness/ and the heaviness and the vexation/ that it suffered day and night,/ had made it become very icteric/ and become slim and pale./ Never anyone born to such a martyrdom/ was put nor had such anger/ as it seemed to have./ I believe that no one could/ do to it anything that could please it/ nor that it would want to withdraw/ nor be comforted under any condition/ from the pain that it had in its heart.

In Guillaume's view, sadness is incompatible with a religion of love because it suppresses the motivational forces that drive the subject to interact with the opposite sex:

> Il ne li tenoit d'anvoiser,
> Ne d'acoler ne de baiser,
> Car qui le cuer a bien dolant,
> Sachiez de voir qu'il n'a talant
> De joer ne de queroler.
> Nus ne se porroit amoler
> Qui duel auroit, de joie faire
> Car Joie et duel sont dui contraire. [33]

She did not care for amusing herself,/ nor for embracing or kissing,/because the one whose heart is aching a lot,/ you must know in truth that he has no interest / in amusement or dancing./ None could be moved,/ among those having pain, to be merry/ because happiness and pain are two opposite things.

From the vantage point of courtly erotic literature, inactivity or idleness did not constitute a *per se* disturbing element of mental pain. They were not listed among the negative features characterizing sadness. On the contrary, the disinterest in productive activity represented the most typical condition of the aristocratic class and of the followers of this tradition of courtly love. In the allegoric construction by Guillaume, the guardian of the access to the garden of Deduit is *Oiseuse,* a word which means idle; also, a large amount of time and emotional resources were devoted to the rites of beauty and love, perquisites for the practice of courtly love:

«Je me faz, dist ele, oiseouse
Apeler a mes quenoïssanz;
Riche fame suis et puissanz,
S'ai d'une chose mout bon tens,
Car a nule rien je n'entens
Qu' a moi joer et solacier
et a moi pignier et trecier.[34]

I let me – she said – idle/ be called by my acquaintances;/ I am a rich and powerful woman,/ and if I have a lot of time for a happy thing,/ it is because I spend my time in nothing else/ than in amusing and entertain myself / and in combing and plaiting my hair.

The Dignity of Acedia

Dante Alighieri's *Divine Comedy* was composed about a century later, at the beginning of 1300, in Florence, a society dominated by a mercantile and financial bourgeoisie which was undergoing a period of breath-taking expansion. With his *Comedia*, Dante proposed to create a map of the entire human condition and so to identify all of the devilish or spiritual forces operating within the society and the individual. Ethical reflection on acedia could therefore not be omitted.

In Dante's ultra-mundane universe *accidiosi* were located both among the damned of Hell and the penitents of Purgatory. In the fourth circle of Dante's Purgatory *accidiosi* espy "negligenza e indugio/ da noi per tepidezza in ben far messo" ("negligence and delay /by us in well doing put.") [35] According to the law of *contrapasso*,[36] which connects the guilt to its punishment within Dante's conceptualization of the afterlife, souls which are prone to acedia during this life fall prey, after their bodily death, to a penitential haste bordering on the grotesque:

Tosto fur sovr'a noi, perché correndo
si movea tutta quella turba magna;

e due dinanzi gridavan piangendo:
  «Maria corse con fretta a la montagna;
e Cesare per soggiogare Ilerda,
punse Marsilia e poi corse in Ispagna».
  «Ratto, ratto, che 'l tempo non si perda
per poco amor», gridavan li altri appresso,
«che studio di ben far grazia rinverda».[37]

Rapidly they were upon us, as running/ that big crowd moved on;/ and two in
front of the others shouted as they cried:/ 'Mary ran in a hurry to the moun-
tain;/ and in order to conquer Ilerda, Caesar stabbed Marseilles and then ran to
Spain'./ 'Fast, fast, so that the time will not be wasted/ for lack of love', shouted the others behind them, 'as the effort of doing well makes grace green again

In Dante's view, then, the element which most antithetically characterizes the
sin of acedia is slowness and the slowing down of goal-directed activities. The
rise of Florentine trading and manufacturing bourgeoisie was associated with an
ever increasing attention towards the time needed for implementing productive
activities, a key factor in effectiveness and competitive performance (Le Goff,
1960). It is therefore not surprising that within such framework the slowness
with which admittedly spiritual tasks were completed, has become the hallmark
of the sin of acedia.

However, in his description of the expiation of *accidiosi,* Dante's phantasy
creates a situation which is also not altogether lacking in comical traits: *accidiosi* are overcome by sacred zeal to the point that they are unable to communicate
with Dante as a pilgrim and cannot even comply with the most elementary social norms of salutation and conversation.

We know that Dante's father, although he belonged to the aristocracy, practiced usury (Piattoli, 1950). Dante was always extremely severe in his judgment
of this kind of financial activity and generally maintained a critical attitude towards the ethical values of the Florentine bourgeoisie. The accidiosi's gro-
tesquely fast pace seem to disguise an implicit empathy for the sin they commit-
ted during their earthly life. And, incidentally, it was in the fourth ring of
Purgatory that Dante himself displayed increased somnolence:

  Poi quando fuor da noi tanto divise
quell'ombre, che veder più non potersi,
novo pensiero dentro a me si mise,
  del qual più altri nacquero e diversi;
e tanto d'uno in altro vaneggiai,
che gli occhi per vaghezza ricopersi,
  e'l pensamento in sogno trasmutai.[38]

Then when they were from us so far divided/ those shadows, that they could
not be seen any more,/ a new thought pushed itself up within me,/ and from
that other and different ones were born;/ and to such an extent I raved from one

to another,/ so that my eyes I covered due to sleepiness,/ and changed the thought into the dream.

As the reader will remember, somnolence, the inability to concentrate on manual and intellectual activities were among the most notable characteristics of Evagrius's acedia. Dante seems then to implicitly admit that he identifies with the *accidiosi* of the Purgatory; he even claim to be one of them. And the admission of this identification appears particularly illuminating with reference to the representation of them that he gives in the first *Cantica* of *Commedia*.

In the third ring of Hell *accidiosi* lie in the Stygian Swamp, beside the Wrathful, but they pay for their guilt under water:

> e anche vo' che tu per certo credi
>   che sotto l'acqua è gente che sospira,
> e fanno pullular quest'acqua al summo,
> come l'occhio ti dice, u' che s'aggira.
>   Fitti nel limo dicon: "tristi fummo
> ne l'aere dolce che dal sol s'allegra,
> portando dentro accidïoso fummo:
>   or ci attrristiam ne la belletta negra".
> Quest'inno si gorgoglian ne la strozza,
> ché dir nol posson con parola integra». [39]

and I also want that you believe for truth/ that there are people breathing under the water,/ and that they make this water above bubble,/ as your eye can tell you, wherever it moves./ Thrust in the mud they say: "sad were we/ in the sweet air rejoicing from the sun, bringing within us the smoke of acedia:/ now we are sad in the black mud"./ This anthem do they gurgle in their throat,/ as they can not pronounce it with a complete word.

Sharply juxtaposed to the bestial ferocity of the Wrathful, to the violent humiliation implicit in the muddy and degrading environment in which they pay for their sins, is the tact with which the poet states the accidiosi's sentence. The quoted verse summarize in the icasticity of an obituitarial epigram the dire fate of guilt and damnation. To these accidiosi, Dante pays his respects: he feels he is at least in part one of them.

The *Commedia* therefore reflects the dispute between pauperism and the bourgeois value of effectiveness which dominated the later part of Middle Ages in Italy and elsewhere. It also found religious and cultural expression in the birth of the order of Minor Friars and subsequently in the fight for survival of the spiritual wing of that movement. Over the next centuries, social transformations became ever more rapid. By this time, the feudal productive system was in decline, even though the development of trading and urban classes went on incessantly all across Europe. Acedia tended to be characterized more and more as a form of guilty inaction, a character trait more loosely associated with religious practice.[40]

A Threat to "Gooded Temporales"

The last of the *Canterbury Tales,* written by Geoffrey Chaucer (a man with a particular talent for business as well) gives obvious evidence of such a process. Among the pilgrims going to Canterbury, the Parson is the last to speak. He does not offer them a story, but a sermon about penitence and mortal sins. Among these sins, according to the tradition, we find acedia.

The parson's description of acedia retains significant affective components. Sadness, as well as desperation, are listed among the vices flowing from it. Again, in line with tradition, with reference to the semantic notion of inaction, he stresses that acedia is, above all, an obstacle to undertaking spiritual activities. But in Chaucer's ethical reflection the negative consequences of acedia are in no way limited to the man's spiritual life:

> Now certes this foule synne Accidie is eek a ful greet enemy to the liflode of the body, for it ne hath no purveaunce agayn temporeel necessitee, for it forsleweth and forsluggeth and destroyeth alle gooded temporales by reccheleesnesse.[41]

And again, with reference to poor control over the activity of a man's subordinates: "Of this comth poverte and destruccioun, bothe of spiritueel and temporeel thynges." [42]

The concept of acedia was thus making a decisive turn in its more than thousand year long journey, moving farther and farther away from the experience of mental pain and to carry with it messages and prescriptions more relevant to social organization. And, this, in turn, moved it essentially outside the field of the present study. What is obviously relevant to this study is the first phase of this conceptual journey, when the sin of *acedia vel tristitia* represented the prevailing paradigm for mental pain related experiences.

Social Attitudes Towards Mental Pain and the Experience of Saint Paul

For over a thousand years, sadness was considered a vice or capital sin for the whole Christendom. Yet, we are at a loss when trying to understand the foundations of this judgment in light of the evangelical precept of love. In the Sermon on the Mount, Jesus stated: "μακάριοι οἱ πενθοῦντες,/ ὅτι αὐτοὶ παρακληθήσονται" [43] and, again, in a different context: "Δεῦτε πρὸς με πάντες οἱ κοπιῶντες καὶ περφορτισμένοι, κἀγὼ ἀναπαύσω ὑμᾶς." [44] Nor were acedia or sadness included in the list of vices Saint Paul mentioned in his letter to Galatians.[45]

The moral damnation associated with sadness was widely accepted in pagan philosophy. But, how did it find its way into Christian reflection? Can we simply explain such long lasting phenomenon in terms of the passive assimilation of pagan models which were prevalent during the early and formative period of the Christian era?

If there is some sign of uneasiness with respect to mental pain to be found in the New Testament, it is likely to be in the Letters by Saint Paul. Cassianus was acutely aware of this. In his Second Letter to the Corinthians, Paul talked about his suffering and the danger of the violent death from which he had recently escaped. Two concepts guided his reflection: λύπη and παράκλησις (*pain* and *consolation*). And he made clear that the sharing of his experience of persecution with the brothers from Corinth and Achaia was for him a great source of consolation.

However, the letter follows a previous exchange, including another letter which is no longer extant. About such a letter, sent by Paul to the Corinthians some time before 2 Cor, he writes:

ἐκ γὰρ πολλῆς θλίψεως καὶ συνοχῆς καρδίας ἔγραψα ὑμῖν διὰ πολλῶν δακρύων, οὐχ ἵνα λυπηθῆτε ἀλλὰ τὴν ἀγάπην ἵνα γνῶτε ἣν ἔχω περισσοτέρως εἰς ὑμᾶς[46]

In fact I wrote to you because of severe affliction and anguish of heart among many tears, not with the aim of hurting you, but so that you can know the extraordinary love I have towards you.

Inferring from the general context of the letter, Saint Paul's συνοχὴ καρδίας is likely to be related to the space the Corinthians granted to some of his unnamed adversaries. We cannot here reconstruct in detail this delicate relational issue between the apostle and his flock. Rather we wish to underscore that Paul had apparently been accused of having shared his sadness to his followers, therefore inducing or transmitting to them a similar affect. And from such an imputation he tried to defend himself:

Ὅτι εἰ καὶ ἐλύπησα ὑμᾶς ἐν τῇ ἐπιστολῇ, οὐ μεταμέλομαι· εἰ καὶ μεταμελόμην, βλέπω [γάρ] ὅτι ἡ ἐπιστολὴ ἐκείνη εἰ καί πρὸς ὥραν ἐλύπησεν ὑμᾶς, νῦν χαίρω, οὐχ ὅτι ἐλυπήθητε ἀλλ᾽ ὅτι ἐλυπήθητε εἰς μετάνοιαν.[47]

Because, even if I have hurt you with the letter, I do not regret it: even if I had regretted it, I see [in fact] that even if at the time that letter hurt you I now rejoice, not because you have been hurt but because you have been hurt for your conversion

We can infer that, within Paul's social and cultural environment, namely, that of the imperial age of the Greek cities, sadness, the pain of the mind, was not completely approved of. Above all, the communication of such suffering (the letter of tears), seems to have been stigmatized by the Corinthians as reproachable. In the face of such a collective attitude, Saint Paul was evidently put on the defensive. He speaks about a worldly sadness, but apparently only with the aim of stressing its opposite, namely, the regenerative role of sadness understood in theological context. Paul is not in a position to refute, from an ethical point of view, the assumption that emotional pain is a substantially unacceptable affect, because it was felt to be so in the society in which he carried out his pastoral mission. Rather, he explains that the expression of one's own pain was to be deemed justified in light of the aim of conversion.

Saint Paul had to defend himself against the charge of having transmitted emotional pain to his brothers. But, in the anthropology and ethics of late-antique, and, subsequently, in the Medieval Church, sadness came to be qualified as a devilish inclination. Cassianus interpreted Saint Paul's statements about λύπη κατὰ κόσμον as having a biblical basis. But, this is an an evident distortion. And, any attempt to reconcile this position with the evangelical message appears problematic.

Thomas Aquinas's Rational Approach to the Sin of Sadness

Jesus' εὐαγγέλιον had been characterized by an extremely open attitude towards human physical and mental pain. While the theology of late-antiquity and the early Medieval period was easily able to overlook the existing contradictions between ethics of the church and the New Testament, or, to be satisfied with reliance on some vaguely consistent scriptural quotation, the thirteenth century systematic theologian, Thomas Aquinas, was not able to rest content with mere analogies.

The founder of Scholasticism aimed at building a consistent theological system, based on the assumption that faith and reason were mutually reinforcing. In the *Questiones disputatae de malo,* his reflection on capital vices identified a specific criterion that enabled him to differentiate and categorize human desires from an ethical perspective.

Thomas located such criterion in the impact that each of them has on the relationship between man and God. God, too, is the object of human desire and emotion. Even in the context of the introjected relation with the *Summum Bonum,* man expresses at least *in potentia* tendencies which are written within the configuration of his soul. God, as far as he is the *Summum Bonum,* is the authentic and natural object of any human appetite. Every appetite of the human personality can then be judged as good or bad on the basis of its relationship with the most important love object.

> Unde et in omni peccato dicuntur esse duo, scilicet conversio ad commutabile bonum et auersio a bono incommutabili.[48]

> Therefore in addition two elements are said to exist in every sin, i.e. movement towards a changeable good and a movement away from the unchangeable good.

In Aquinas's view, vices are therefore only desires or life habits that propel man away from the *Summum Bonum.* From this perspective, not much space is left for damnation or conceptualization as guilt of experiences which cause emotional pain. However, on the Thomistic approach, the integration of theoretical reflections within the tradition of the church was an essential requirement of theoretical formulations. Specifically, he could not in any way think of reshaping the list of capital sins handed down by the Church to his society. So, in order to solve this aporia, Thomas had to redefine, i.e. reduce, the semantic field of the vice of acedia. This he did in a single sentence: "Accidia autem est tedium vel tristitia boni spiritualis et interni." [49]

Acedia, on this new meaning, was only sadness and lack of interest specifically referring to religious experience. From the Thomstic perspective, acedia cannot easily be conceptualized, either as low productivity in the economic field or in reference to work life, nor can it be said to be associated with states of prostration and desperation. The latter may be differently motivated or basically unexplainable. Thomas even thought acedia was a capital sin only if it was met with voluntary adherence on the part of man's soul:

> Peccatum autem per se et proprie est in uoluntate ut dicit Augustinus. Et ideo si accidia nominet actum uoluntatis refugientis internum et spirituale bonum, potest habere perfectam rationem peccati, si uero accipiatur prout est actus appetitus sensitiui non habet rationem peccati nisi ex uoluntate, in quantum scilicet talis motus potest a uoluntate prohiberi: unde si non prohibetur habet aliquam rationem peccati set imperfectam. [50]

> The sin *per se* and properly lies in the will, as Augustinus says. And therefore if acedia refers to the act of will fleeing from the inner and spiritual good, it can have a perfect quality of sin, but if we refer with it to the act of the sensitive appetite it does not have the quality of a sin unless it has it due to the will, scilicet as far as such a move can be prohibited by the will: and therefore, if it is not prohibited it has some quality of a sin, although not a perfect one.

If acedia is lack of interest in God, its essentially sinful nature is finally demonstrated in terms of rational thinking. This was acknowledged by a modern philosopher when he reviewed the history of the condition (Colapietro, 1997). But, over the course of this conceptual shift, acedia became something markedly different from what it had been traditionally thought to be. In other words, the same *sign* was now referring to a different *thing*. No longer did it mean silent apathy or long-lasting suffering, but, instead, subtle hostility towards God and his love. For Aquinas, acedia is not the representation of a frequent and socially relevant emotional experience.

The impact of the Thomistic conceptualization on pastoral practice would be limited, but, with the end of Middle Ages, acedia would cease to be a valued instrument for thinking and communicating about the relation between society and the painful experiences of the individual. Within the vice of acedia "the neglect-idleness-indolence aspect became more and more the focus; and the trend toward the use of sloth and related terms became more predominant." [51] With the Reformation, concern for one's own earthly tasks and productivity would clearly come to the fore in society. Pain and hopelessness would come to be associated with humoral medicine and medical theory.

NOTES

1. Diogenes Laertius, *De vitis et dogmatibus clarorum philosophorum*, VII, 110-112.
2. Epictetus, *Enchiridion*, 5.
3. Epictetus, *Enchiridion*, 1.
4. Epictetus, *Enchiridion*, 11.
5. Epictetus *Enchiridion*, 16.
6. Jackson, 1986, p. 65-77.
7. *Practicos*, X, 1.
8. *Practicos*, X, 2-5.
9. *De coenobiorum institutis*, Col. 360.
10. Ibidem, Col. 358.
11. Ibidem.
12. Guillamont, 1971, p. 84.
13. *Moralia in Iob.* Vol. 76, Coll. 620C-621B.
14. *Practicos*, 12, 4-16.
15. Ibidem, 12, 2-4.
16. The monk's expectations are so intense that "ἔτρισεν ἡ θύρα, κἀκεῖνος ἐξήλλατο, φωνῆς ἤκουσε, καὶ διὰ τῆς θυρίδος παρεκύψε" From, Evagrius Ponticus, *De Octo Spiritibus Malitiae*, Col. 1159B.
17. The term *projective identification* refers to an omnipotent phantasy through which a given emotional mental content is projected *inside* the object's mental apparatus (*cfr.* Melanie Klein, 1946).
18. *Practicos*, 16, 1-2.
19. Ibidem, 27, 1-7.
20. *De coenobiorum institutis*, Col 397, A-B.
21. *Practicos*, 29, 1-7.
22. Ibidem.
23. *De coenobiorum institutis*, Col. 363A.
24. Evagrius Ponticus, *De octo spiritibus malitiae*, Col. 1159B.
25. *De coenobiorum institutis*, Col 367.
26. Ibidem. Col. 375 A.
27. 1 Thess. 2: 9.
28. 2 Thess. 3:10.
29. *De coenobiorum institutis*, Col 370.
30. *Moralia in Job*, Vol. 76, Coll. 620-622.
31. Casagrande e Vecchio, 2000, pp. 78-95; see also Jackson, 1986, pp. 65-77.
32. *Roman de la rose*, VV. 291-310.
33. Ibidem, VV. 331-338.
34. Ibidem, VV. 582-588.
35. *Inferno*, XVIII, VV. 107-108.
36. This might be rendered as *corresponding retaliation*.

37. *Purgatorio*, XVIII, VV. 97-105.
38. Ibidem, VV 139-145.
39. *Inferno*, VII, VV. 117-126.
40. Jackson, 1986, p. 73.
41. *The Canterbury Tales*, X, I, 684.
42. Ibidem, X, I, 721.
43. Mt 5:4.
44. Mt 11:28.
45. Gal. 5:19-21.
46. 2 Cor. 2:4
47. 2 Cor. 7:8-9.
48. *Questiones Disputatae De Malo*, q.8, a.1, ad. 1.
49. Ibidem.
50. Ibidem, q. 11, a.1.
51. Jackson, 1986, p. 75.

Chapter Three
Sadness and Human Societies

SADNESS: THE ILLNESS OF OUR TIME

Let us now return to depression. And, let us also return to the present time. In the second half of the last century, depression was the object of a deep interest at different levels. DSM psychiatric nosography ranked alterations of mood higher in terms of diagnostic status than it did alterations of perceptions and ideation. Since the United States was previously influenced by the Bleulerian diagnostic tradition, this shift implied that many instances previously classified as cases of schizophrenia were now placed in the diagnostic category of mood disorders. Admissions for affective disorders increased over the period 1950-1980 in contrast to the preceding three decades (Angst, 1984). In France, according to data from CREDES, rates for depression increased by 50% between the beginning of the 1980s and the beginning of 1990s (Le Pape and Lecomte, 1996). The introduction of new anti-depressive compounds into the pharmaceutical market starting in the mid-1970s–compounds which had a much more favorable tolerability profile than the previously developed triciclic–was associated with a breath-taking increase in prescriptions for this kind of drug. In France, between 1975 and 1984 the quantity of antidepressants prescribed by the general practitioner increased by 300% [1] fluoxetina having been the second most often prescribed drug there in 1995.[2]

This escalation in prescribing such medications is undoubtedly tied to a higher awareness of the epidemiological scope and dangers of depressive disorders among physicians. And anti-depressive drugs could not have been so massively successful unless a high level of information had been made available to the general population, or, in the absence of a conspicuous sensitivity on their part to the problem of diagnosis and treatment of depressive disorders.

Depression has been described as a fashionable disease (Bergeret, 1976). Since 1966, there has been a proliferation of articles on various types of depression in, for example, magazines for women, like the French *Elle* [3]. Also, books on depression and on drugs useful for treating it have been met with great success among the general public (*e.g.* Kramer, 1993). We ought not therefore be astonished if nowadays in Italy a successful pop band decides to identify itself with a name that makes reference to a widely used antidepressant compound.

Depression seems to now enjoy extraordinary success as a model for conceptualizing pain of mind. But we need to beware of the fact that the increasing rate of prevalence of depressive disorders in our society does not seem to be merely the effect of a reorientation of diagnostic styles. Based on the evidence available at the end of the 1980s (Klerman & Weissman, 1989), evidence which indicated an increase in rates of depression in cohorts born after World War II, an international research project (Cross-National Collaborative Group, 1992) conducted a direct analysis of time trends of major depression. It drew on homogeneous methodologies in nine countries spanning three continents. All of the test subjects were evaluated according to analogous diagnostic criteria (DSM-III or RDC). The study results indicated a progressive increase in the prevalence of major depression in younger cohorts in all of the countries in which tests were conducted. This means that the differences observed between rates identified in different cohorts must be interpreted, at least in part, as an expression of changes which are currently taking place in those human populations addressed by this study, and that they ought not be interpreted with respect to the criteria according to which they had been evaluated.

While the frequency of cases of depression is rising across the world populations, its relevance is also being given greater attention not only among clinicians, but also in society at large. There seems to exist an enigmatic tie between depression and the conditions of life in contemporary society. Alain Ehrenberg authoritatively stated that depression expresses in a paradigmatic way the existential difficulties experienced by the individual in the twentieth century. Contemporary man, so he claims, has worked himself free from the moral imperatives which imprisoned previous generations and is compelled to contend with the responsibility of autonomously managing his own life:

> In summary, rules seem to have radically changed, whichever field is considered—business, school, family. No more obedience, discipline, adherence to the prevailing ethics, but rather flexibility, readiness to change, speed in adaptation etc. Self-mastery, psychic and affective ductility, skill in acting and reacting make everyone feel obliged to permanently adapt to a world which is in fact losing his permanence, an unstable and provisional world, with flows and pathways bouncing like the many teeth of a malicious cogwheel. Even the sociopolitical scene has become difficult to read. These institutional transformations transmit a feeling of confusion, the feeling that everyone, even the most humble and simple ones, must take the burden of *choosing everything* and *deciding on everything*.[4]

In this altered social reality, depression becomes the prototype of human suffering because "it embodies the tension between the longing to be simply oneself and the difficulty to be oneself."[5]

DEPRESSION: AN ILLNESS FOR EVERY ERA

Nowadays, Western physicians and society are looking at depression with new interest. And the disease has become more widely dispersed throughout the population. But the history of this illness and of other conditions of emotional suffering, which we have summarized above, gives us cause to carefully consider these transformations which the disease has undergone as well as the ways in which it is perceived.

Depression seems to have been present in Western society as long as documentation of it has been available. Some basic characteristics of the disorders were described in the *Corpus Hipppocraticum*, or in works produced in ensuing centuries. Scientific texts were specifically devoted to melancholy in antiquity and late antiquity as well as in the context of Mediaeval Arabic medicine, the Renaissance, the Enlightenment, after the French Revolution and again in the period of positivistic science. No age, with the seeming exception of the early Christian Middle Ages, has totally disregarded it. Instead, interest in understanding depression has periodically extended beyond the limits of the medical community and reached to people in both upper and lower classes. Periodically, it came to be thought of as a fashionable disease, particularly among the educated people.

Aristotle believed that melancholic temperaments possessed peculiar intellectual virtues[6]; the fifteenth century Neoplatonic philosopher, Marsilio Ficino, held a similar view [7]. *The Anatomy of Melancholy* by Robert Burton is also evidence of a deep interest on the part of the Elizabethan culture in melancholy, one which would become one of the sources for the composition of Shakespeare's *Hamlet*. In the eighteenth century, English poets recognized in melancholy the distinctive mark of a sensitive and refined soul[8]. The list of the close interrelations between history of culture and history of melancholy could continue at length. Further references are to be found in Jackson (1986), and in *Saturn and Melancholy* by Klibansky, Panofsky & Saxl (1964).

Even if depression and its representation have elicited the interest of wider areas of Western society, it does not seem to me that this amounts to a new way of cognitively and emotionally working through personal problems, one which is peculiar and specific to the society in which we are now living, owing to the development of less normative or rigid family structures.

On the other hand, one element which undoubtedly differentiates our society from those of antiquity as well as from nineteenth century society, is the enormous diffusion and high level of medical expertise available to all strata of society. In the ancient world, theoretical insights and physicians' expertise and practice were available only to the higher classes; the success in distribution of medical services over the last 200 years has been continuous and overwhelming. And, given this development, depression has become more widespread. In other words, depression and medicine seem to be linked by an implicit and invisible knot.

Our historical review (see Ch. 1) has underscored the fact that melancholy, of which modern depression represents a version that is more precisely differentiated from other emotional conditions, came into being when physicians of the fourth century B.C. established a connection between pain (δυσθυμίη) and an altered *crasis* of body humors (τὸ μελανχολικόν). Undoubtedly, the medicine of antiquity and late antiquity enriched the understanding of melancholic states with its grasp of important details. After the long suspension of creative thinking in the Middle Ages and the Renaissance, nineteenth century medicine became progressively more able to differentiate the two components of melancholic states: sadness and fear. It was thus able to anticipate the most widely accepted classification in contemporary psychiatry.

However, the 2400 years which have followed since the composition of the *Corpus Hippocraticum* did not produce any evidence which could definitely provide an empirical foundation for the *aphorism* VI, XXIII. No twentieth century physician was able to establish an unquestionable link between prolonged pain and the alteration of bodily humors or to any other relevant principle of human bodily functioning.

Evidence regarding the role of neurotransmitters in the etiology of depression dates back to the second half of last century; however, our knowledge of the relation between functioning of the brain and states of deep or long lasting sadness still remains rather rudimentary. Biological psychiatry continues to claim that the cause of depression is currently unknown.[9]

The hypothesis that assumes there is a link between the depressive disease and alterations of brain neurotransmission is largely based on the observation that catecolamin re-uptake inhibitors are an effective treatment for depression. Recently, however, the effectiveness of anti-depressive drug treatment, or at least its superiority to psychotherapeutic treatments, has been authoritatively challenged (Fisher e Greenberg, 1997). The lack of a sound empirical basis for the catecolaminergic theory of depression, as well as the frequent variations in such theory over time have created in researchers outside the field of clinical psychiatry the feeling that this is a science which is "turning around itself."[10]

We are not discussing here the strength of empirical evidence currently supporting the existence of a tie between body functioning and mind pain. What struck us deeply, however, while studying the history of depression in Western society and medicine, was the gap, the wide distance between the formulation of such a theory and the real possibility, or even the appearance of an interest in putting such an hypothesis to an empirical test. For thousands of years, depression has been described and classified, without even discussing its status as an illness. Apparently, the development of medical science seemed to imply, or even rest on, the assumption that sustained mental pain is a morbid condition.

However, the historical outline presented here has shown how melancholy and depression were not the only socially relevant paradigms for representing particularly intense and prolonged mental pain. It is clear that, from an historical point of view, at least two additional paradigms were met with a wide and long lasting consensus: that of guilt and that of error. For the Stoic philosophers, pain was chiefly due to an error in judgment. For the church, *tristitia* was an evil disposition of the man's soul.

These three different paradigms met with different levels of successes through the history of Western society. In fact, in the early Middle Ages, the paradigm of melancholy basically came to be overshadowed in terms of any meaningful impact it might have had on large strata of society, only to resurface in the Renaissance. The paradigm of error was similarly acknowledged in antiquity, but did not reappear at the end of the Middle Ages. It was authoritatively claimed that cognitive psychotherapy, which nowadays enjoys wide acceptance, particularly as a treatment for depressive syndromes, extensively embodied the principles of the Stoic ethics. Finally, the paradigm of guilt dominated the approaches to the analysis of mental pain since the age of Gregorius Magnus till the end of the Middle Ages.

In essence, the paradigm of illness met with varied consensus over the centuries. Assessment of it very closely followed the development of Western medicine. With the early development of medicine, melancholy entered into the Greek cultural scenario, lost its status in the Dark Ages when medical science declined, and then reappeared again when medicine emerged from obscurity at the close of the Middle Ages. Given the extraordinary and unquestioned social standing of modern medicine, the analysis of depressive disorders is now publically legitimated to a much greater degree than heretofore.

But, again, we must beware of the tendency to confound social consensus and socially diffused practices. Depression has found its way into psychiatric textbooks, as well as magazines, pharmacies as well as television programs. But this does not mean that the medical model for representing mental pain is the only one, or even the prevailing one, in therapeutic practice, nor is it always the existential choice of individuals in the twentieth and twenty-first centuries. In fact, it has been shown that many depressed subjects do not seek or receive anti-depressive drug treatment (Keller et al., 1982).

Druss et al. (2000) published the results of an important study on the epidemiology of treatments for depression. The authors examined a population of about 7500 subjects using the Diagnostic Interview Survey, an instrument of proven reliability. This was done within the framework of the third National Health and Nutrition Examination Survey (1988-1994). In this population, 312 individuals (4.1%) were affected by a major depressive disorder at the time the data were collected. Only 23 subjects, (7.4% of patients suffering from major depression in the sample), were receiving anti-depressive medication. Can this be attributed to poor diagnostic or therapeutic competence on the part of the treating physicians? Perhaps. But, this might not be the only reason, particularly given that nearly 80% of untreated depressed subjects had not even talked about their own state to the treating physicians. They did not feel that their own emotional pain, undoubtedly deep and long-lasting, should be brought to the attention of a physician.

DEPRESSION AS A SOCIAL DEFENSE MECHANISM

Representing or communicating experiences of pain within the family or social relationship framework is a complex process. Over the course of time, Western culture has produced several paradigms which aim at organizing and transmitting these painful experiences. The everyday psychiatric practice confirms that these paradigms are frequently shared by patients and their relatives, who often speak about their own or a relative's state of suffering as either a disease for which they seek the help of a physician, or a guilt, for which they accuse themselves or the patient (many studies on the emotional reactions evoked by depressed patients in their more or less close family environment are indicative of this [11]), or an error, an incorrect interpretation of an absolutely pleasant life condition.

Pain can hardly leave us unmoved. Some rudimentary form of identification ties us emotionally to the human beings who surround us, no matter how primitive or contiguous-autistic (Ogden, 1989) or narcissistic the prevailing organization of our mind may be. At some level, therefore, the pain of our fellow human beings hurts us and the pain we feel provokes in us an emotional response: anger.

Our mind tries then to defend itself as far as it can from this disturbing experience and from the anger directed towards those who are suffering. The basic defensive move is then *negation* or *denial.* Our relative's pain is no longer the expression of suffering, of violence or loss, but rather an unmotivated emotion, due to a blurred awareness or even to a subtly perverted will. Hostility, devaluation, and projection blend together with the primitive defenses described here earlier, and thus produce a representation of the suffering individual which allows us to emotionally distance ourselves from him and, if possible, to express towards him part of the anger and the helplessness that the situation elicits from us.

Social representations of the experience of pain can obtain wide consensus in so far as they reflect more or less meaningful facets of private experience. Depression, sadness as a disease, significantly meets this requirement. It allows the sufferer some rights: rights to assistance, to lamenting, to specialized care. But, at the same time, it defines suffering as a pathological process, an inadequate representation of events, one which lacks a basis in reality.

Depression also involves a devaluation of the experience of pain: it is not an experience of *reality* but a *dysfunction* of mind. It also involves a de-animation of pain: suffering is treated as an incorrect response to information coming in from the environment. These processes offer the unquestionable advantage of protecting the patient's relatives and, to a certain degree, the more superficial components of the patient's own personality, because they act as a barrier which reduces the dangers implied in too deep an identification with suffering.

These are the reasons for the success of this concept of depression, particularly manifest and perceivable as it is in an age like ours, which is extremely fearful of human emotions and relations. However, it is precisely because it amounts to a defensive and partial representation of the experience of pain that depression will continue to be in some way and for many people an unsatisfactory paradigm. It will therefore continue to be challenged by other competing analyses and ideologies of human pain.

NOTES

1. Ehrenberg, 1998[1999], p. 196.
2. Ibidem, p. 250.
3. Ibidem, p. 156.
4. Ibidem, p. 251.
5. Ibidem, p. 185.
6. *Problemata Physica*, XXX, 1.
7. *De Triplici Vita*, 1489.
8. Sickels, 1932.
9. APA, 2000a, pp. 352-353; also 371; See also Stefanis & Stefanis, 1999, p. 2.
10. Ehrenberg, 1998[1999], p. 245.
11. Klerman et al., 1984, pp. 62-63.

Part II
Clinical Facts

Chapter Four
Looking through a Distortive Mirror: Descriptive Psychopathology of Depression from a Psychoanalytic Perspective

DEPRESSION AS AN OBJECT OF OBSERVATION

Multiple Treatment Options

A wide range of therapeutic options is currently available to the psychiatrist for treating depression; the efficacy of most of them has been empirically proved. Selective serotonin re-uptake inhibitors have now been added to the existing list of triciclic anti-depressants. And, more recently, still more non-triciclic compounds have been brought to the market, some of them having a double action, i.e. on both the serotoninergic and the noradrenergic system. Lastly, compounds which act selectively on noradrenalin re-uptake are also now available.

Through different mechanisms, these compounds are all believed to increase catecolamin availability at the level of the CNS synapses; at the same time, they have a much lower risk of inducing severe or life-threatening side effects than do the triciclic medications. The list of antidepressant drugs might be expanded at length; also, it includes some preparations derived from herbal extracts (Kasper et al., 2008).

The range of available psychological options for treating depression may not be as wide as this, but it has been appreciably expanded over the last few decades. And, there is now substantial empirical evidence to support the claims to effectiveness made by some of them. The foundational study of the National Institute of Mental Health on the outcome of the psychotherapy of depression (Elkin, 1994) has clearly demonstrated that Interpersonal Psychotherapy of Depression (i.e. an interpersonally focused, time-limited dynamic treatment) for those with interpersonal difficulties is distinctly effective in the treatment of mild to moderate major depression. Moreover, the body of empirical evidence supporting cognitive-behavioral therapies is truly impressive (*cfr.* Scott, 2001). Evidence of efficacy is somewhat less sound for behavioral therapies and short-term dynamic therapies (Roth & Fonagy, 1996; more favorable data is available in Cujpers et al., 2007).

Psychological treatment for depression undoubtedly antedates the empirical approach to the evaluation of treatments. Freud's earlier and substantial contribution to the study of depression dates back to 1917. A moderate theoretical interest in the psychogenesis of depression has been perceivable throughout the history of the psychoanalytic movement. In a previous article, we reviewed main psychoanalytical models of depression and discussed their contribution to clinical practice (Azzone, 2001).

In sum, many competing approaches to depression exist, and may currently advance one or another claim to evidence of efficacy, even if they rely on very disparate or even opposing theoretical frameworks. In the context of this open-ended debate, a number of authors have underscored the potential benefits of integrating these treatments. Among the advocates of this is Glen Gabbard. He has pointed out the advantages of a psychodynamic approach toward patients who do not respond to somatic treatment or who suffer from a simultaneous personality disorder.[1] Actually, a number of empirical studies has indicated that a combination of medication and psychotherapy can offer advantages over both treatments when they are used in isolation. This is especially true in cases of severe, recurring and chronic Major Depressive Disorders (Jindal & Thase, 2003). However, empirical literature is clearly not univocal on this issue and recently an intense debate has developed around the role of unaccompanied psychological treatment as a first-choice for major depressive episodes (Fisher & Greenberg, 1997).

At a level which more closely approximates the needs for clinical management of depressive symptoms, Karasu (1990 a & b) proposed to select what he took to be the most appropriate of the various psychological and somatic treatments for depression on the basis of each single patient's prevailing symptoms. He also factors into this selection process the specific goals he has set for the treatment. Karasu believes, for instance, that medication is more suited for symptoms such as "psychotic thinking, especially persecutory or nihilistic delusions and auditory hallucinations," while at the same time assuming that "persistent irrational beliefs that reflect negative distortion or exaggeration, but not psychosis" would be more responsive to psychotherapeutic treatments.[2].

Similarly, Karasu suggests selecting the most apt among the range of available psychological treatments on the basis of the patient's core symptoms and his personality features. Under this perspective, "chronic, pervasive low self-esteem and dejection and excessive feelings of guilt, especially in patients with severe real losses, extended separation in childhood, or long-standing unresolved conflicts related to attachment and loss in early relationships"[3] would require a psychodynamic treatment, while patients with an increased "need of strong guidance and direction" would benefit most from cognitive therapy.[4]

Karasu's model certainly has some appealing features, including the capacity to minimize potential conflicts between the organizations or groups with which mental health professionals identify themselves. However, empirical literature does not seem to confirm such hypotheses. For the time being, to my knowledge, the empirical evidence for the superior efficacy of a single therapeutic approach as applied to selected depressed patient subgroups over others is still limited (APA, 2000b).

Furthermore, the differing approaches to the treatment of depression currently available in the well developed mental health market are not proposed as treatments for particular or specific types of depression. Medication, as well as psychotherapies, rather aims at the treatment of depression in general.

In fact, paradigms of treatment for depression do not reflect the needs of specific patients, but are instead specific *forms of representation* of depressive psychopathology. Like several mirrors, varying in sizes and shapes, they show us an image of a patient, one which includes elements specific to the observational device we are making use of. From this point of view, the problem is not one of summing up or integrating the differing approaches, but rather facilitating meaningful communication between the various mental health workers.

How do these devices work? Through which mental operations do they work on the suffering subject and can they offer to us a representation of him? In what follows, we will try to follow the thread leading from depression to its observers and vice-versa.

Depression as Seen by Observers

The core elements and basic processes inherent in the knowledge of reality have, for over two thousand years, been the object of epistemological investigation. We owe to Immanuel Kant a debt of gratitude for his particularly comprehensive and exhaustive discussion of the philosophical problems implicit in human observational knowledge of the external world. A brief discussion of the principles of Kant's epistemology may therefore be helpful here. It can provide a focus for our efforts at understanding the distortive impact of different paradigms which are relied upon in conceptualizing the various clinical phenomena of depression.

Immanuel Kant (1724-1804), the great German philosopher of the second half of eighteenth century, taught us that knowledge stems from the interaction between the observer and the physical world. In his *Kritik der reinen Vernunft* (1781-1787) Kant investigated the general conditions of human knowledge. As he observed, "Daß alle unsere Erkenntnis mit der Erfahrung anfange, daran ist kein Zweifel;" ("That all knowledge of ours stems from experience is something beyond any doubt;") [5] He argued,

> Wenn ... gleich alle unsere Erkenntnis *mit* der Erfahrung anhebt, so entspringt
> sie darum doch nicht eben alle *aus der* Erfahrung. Denn es könnte wohl sein,
> das selbst unsere Erfahrungserkenntnis ein Zusammengesetztes aus dem sei,

was wir durch Eindrücke empfangen, und dem, was unser eigenes Erkenntnis-
vermögen ... aus sich selbst hergiebt ... [6]

Although [...] any knowledge of ours begins *with* experience, this does not
mean that it comes all *from* experience. In fact, it may well be that even our
empirical knowledge is a composed of what we draw from impressions and of
what our own knoweldge factulty ... gives in itself

Consistent with this perspective, Kant deemed it necessary to distinguish between the objects of knowledge as they exist within the natural world, independently of our knowing activitities, and the objects which we meet within our
experience. He defined the latter as follows: "Der unbestimmte Eigenstand einer empirischen Anschauung heißt Erscheinung." [7] Phenomena, and therefore
the experience which encompasses them, include two components:

In der Erscheinung nenne ich das, was der Empfindung correspondirt, wie Materie derselben, dasjenige aber, welches macht, daß das Mannigfaltige der Er-
schienung in gewissen Verhältnissen geordnet werden kann, nenne ich die
Form der Erscheinung. Da das, worinnen sich die Empfindungen allein ordnen
und in gewisse Form gestellt werden können, nicht selbst wiederum Empfindung sein kann, so ist uns zwar die Materie aller Erscheinung nur *a posteriori*
gegeben, die Form derselben aber muß zu ihnen insgesammt im Gemüthe *a
priori* bereitliegen und daher abgesondert von aller Empfindung können be-
trachtet werden.[8]

In the phenomenon, I term what corresponds to the sensation as its matter; but
I term «form» of the phenomenon whatever makes possible to order the multi-
plicity of the phenomenon within given relationships. Because that in which
only the sensations can be ordered and put in a certain form cannot be a sensation itself, so the matter of any phenomenon is actually given us only *a posteriori*; however, its form must lie in the soul *a priori*, ready, as a whole and then
be able to be considered separately from any sensation.

On Kant's view, the forms of the phenomena are the observer's contribution to
the construction of experiential events. He believed that the primary elements of
this contribution should be the organization of sensory events within the dimensions of time and space. In fact

Der Raum stellt gar keine Eigenschaft irgendeiner Dinge an sich, oder sie in
ihrem Verhältnis aufeinender vor, d.i. keine Bestimmung derselben, die an Eigenständen selbst hastete, und welche bliebe, wenn man auch von allen subjektiven Bedingungen der Anschauung abstrahirte.
        [...] der Raum ist nichts anders, als nur die Forme aller Erscheinungen äu-
ßerer Sinne, d.i. die subjektive Bedingung der Sinnlichkeit, unter der allein uns
äußere Anschauung möglich ist. [9]

The space does not represent at all a property belonging to things in themselves, or to them in their relationship with one another, i.e., it is not at all a de-

termination of themselves, which have itself autonomy, and which would also remain when we abstract from all subjective conditions of intuition.

[...] the space is nothing other than the form of all phenomena of the external senses, i.e the subjective condition of sensibility, under which alone external intuition is possible to us.

Similarly,

Der Zeit ist nicht etwas, was für sich selbst bestände, oder den Dingen als objektive Bestimmung anhinge, mithin übrig bliebe, wenn man von allen subjektiven Bedingungen der Anschauung derselben abstrahirt: [...] die Zeit nichts als die subjektive Bedingung ist, unter der alle Anschauung in uns stattfinden können. [...] Die Zeit ist nichts anders als die Form des innern Sinnes, d.i. des Anschauens unserer selbst und unseres innern Zustandes.[10]

The time is not something which would stand in itself, or which is inherent to the things as an objective determination, and which would therefore persist, should we abstract from all subjective conditions of the intuition itself, [...] the time is nothing other than the subjective condition, under which all intuitions can take place in us. [...] The time is nothing else than the form of the inner sense, i.e. of the intuition of ourselves and of our inner state.

In essence, in Kant's view, knowledge amounts to an interaction between a subject and an object, both are active partners. There is no absolute knowledge of the *das Ding an sich*, of the object as it exists in the objective world outside human experience. As he states:

alle unsre Anschauung nichts als die Vorstellung von Erscheinung sei; das die Dinge, die wir anschauen, nicht das an sich selbst sind, wofür wir sie anschauen, noch ihre Verhältnisse so an sich selbst beschaffen sind, als sie uns erscheinen, und daß, wenn wir unser Subjekt oder auch nur die subjektive Beschaffenheit der Sinne überhaupt ausheben, alle die Beschaffenheit, alle Verhältnisse der Objekte im Raum und Zeit, ja selbst Raum und Zeit verschwinden würden und als Erscheinungen nicht an sich selbst, sondern nur in uns existiren können. Was er für eine Bewandtniß mit den Eigenständen an sich und abgesondert von aller dieser Rezeptivität unserer Sinnlichkeit haben möge, bleibt uns gänzlich unbekannt. Wir kenne nichts als unsere Art, sie wahrzunehmen, die uns eigentümlich ist, die auch nicht notwendig jedem Wesen, ob zwar jedem Menschen, zukommen muß.[11]

[we can say that] all our intuition is nothing else than the representation of the phenomenon; that the things which we intuit are not in themselves what we intuit them for, neither their relations are in themselves shaped so as they appear to us, and that, should we remove our subject, or even only the subjective constitution of the senses in general, all the constitution and all the relations of the objects in space and time, even time and space themselves, would disappear, and that as phenomena they can not exist in themselves, rather only in ourselves. Which could be the condition of the objects in themselves and detached from all this receptivity of our sensibility remains completely unknown to us. We know nothing else than our way of perceiving them which is peculiar to us, and which does not necessarily belong to any being, although it does to any man.

Kant's model of knowledge is particularly rich in suggestions for our present reflection. From his perspective, the observing subject does not enter in direct contact with the thing as such (*das Ding an sich*) i.e. the object as it exists in the external reality, but is rather the product of an interactive process with the subject, hence the term *phenomenon.*

This epistemological perspective can be adopted here as a fruitful metaphor for our efforts at satisfactorily conceptualizing depression. We can state then that while it is obvious that depression consists of a series of events taking place in a sick individual, clinicians and theorists of mental illnesses are able to develop models for such events only in terms of reference theories and specific mental operations peculiar to each of them.

Scientific and professional communication between the various workers involved in the treatment and understanding of depression can be extended only to those representations of depression which can be shared in the context given models.

If clinicians of different backgrounds can and do formulate differing representations of a patient, can we conclude that no meaningful sharing is possible between clinicians who rely on divergent models of mental illness? Psychiatry of the last quarter of the previous century has held that this communication and sharing could be based on a specific model of mental illness, generally referred to as the medical model.

The Utopia of Depression Understood "Objectively"

Throughout the 1960s, the professional identity and practice of psychiatry, then still strongly linked to the institution of the state hospital, was the object of virulent attacks. In his work *Histoire de la folie à l'age classique* (1961), Michel Foucault showed how the precursors of psychiatric hospitals had become widely diffused in sixteenth century Europe chiefly as a response to social control needs, and how, only in subsequent centuries, medical treatment had come to play a central role in the activity and the identity of lunatic asylums. In a still more radical fashion, Szasz (1961) even questioned whether or not mental health disorders could be properly included within the professional and scientific competence of medicine. For him, mental disorders would better be conceptualized as social phenomena, and so not directly connected with the functioning of the body.

These positions obviously posed a threat to the social standing and even the practice of psychiatry as a medical specialty. On the other hand, while such radical theories might well yield useful stimuli for a general restructuring of the psychiatric institution, they offered no real contribution to the treatment, or even handling, of mental disorders in the then dawning context of community-based psychiatric practice.

This climate of radical criticism of psychiatry obviously generated an increasing uneasiness. Many psychiatrists felt the need to reassert the status of psychiatry as a scientific discipline, a position exemplified by Arnold M. Ludwig (1975). According to Ludwig "There can be only one solid foundation for psychiatry, that based on the medical model, and only one legitimate domain of expertise, pertaining to mental illness." The latter would be so defined: "any debilitating cognitive-affective-behavior disorder due primarily to known, suggestive or presumed biological brain dysfunctions, either biochemical or neurophysiological in nature" [12].

The working out of the biomedical point of view, as outlined by Ludwig, immediately posed difficulties in the field of mental health. On the one hand, if one were to reap its full consequences, the option for the biomedical model would have had to imply exclusion "from the concept of mental illness" of a full range of "disorders such as existential problems of living, social adjustment reactions, character disorders, dependency syndromes, existential depressions, and various social deviancy conditions ... since these disorders arise in individuals with presumably intact neurophysiological functioning and are produced primarily by psychosocial variables." [13]

Deprived of any informational resource or device for intervention relevant to psychological and social issues, the psychiatrist would have appeared to be in a position of serious difficulty in interacting with workers coming from different backgrounds; nor could he have proposed to be a leader of institutions or working groups where these differing competences were called to interact reciprocally. Finally, the psychiatrist who relied on a rigid biomedical model could offer very little to the physician operating within other branches of medicine, who generally identifies the psychiatrist as the medical professional most suited to support his medical knowledge with the information and skills that he lacks and who, already in those years, had perceived more and more clearly that a medical theory that focused only on the body, on procedures and equipment, could only respond inadequately to the complex demands of health, which actually rest on a concept of the person as a whole.

George Engel subsequently criticized Ludwig's views in 1977, and termed them reductionistic: "The dominant model of disease [in Ludwig's paper] is biomedical, with molecular biology as its basic scientific discipline. It assumes disease to be fully accounted for by deviations from the norm of measurable biologic (somatic) variables." [14] Engel then proposed to inform the practice of psychiatry by reference to a model he termed *bio-psycho-social.* He meant to underline the importance of psychosocial factors in the genesis, course, consequences and treatment of illness in general, and of mental illness in particular.

However, the term bio-psychosocial should not be misinterpreted. To the three components constituting the model, biological, psychological and social, no parallel status was granted. From Engel's perspective, mental disease has its etiology and pathogenesis in the body. Engel stressed that, from this point of view, schizophrenia and diabetes mellitus "are entirely analogous and ... are appropriately conceptualized within the framework of a medical model of disease." [15] The psychosocial aspects of the bio-psychosocial model allude essentially to factors conditioning the social perception of the illness or potentially interfering with a patient's illness-related behaviors.

The style of synthesis and the formulation of clinical material associated with the bio-psychosocial model has been defined as 'descriptive'; it represents one of the distinguishing features of the diagnostic approach proper to the DSMs system (APA, 1980, 1987, 1994 & 2000a). In the introduction to DSM III, the descriptive approach is explained in terms of an orientation to the description of phenomena, which "attempted to be neutral with respect to theories of etiology" (APA, 2000a, p. XXVI).

As stressed earlier, conceiving of knowledge producing processes as basically passive phenomena is epistemologically untenable. In fact, since the discovery of the personal equation[16], it is well known that, in the natural sciences, the experimenter has an unavoidable impact on observed phenomena.

While DSMs aim at a sort of utopia of a totally objective observation, we are interested in understanding which point of view actually informs the description of depressive disorders which is proposed by DSM-III and DSM-IV. In addition, in the present discussion, we are interested in understanding whether or not such a perspective would allow us to realize a description of phenomena that might prove useful in psychotherapeutic work. Specifically, we are interested in dynamic psychotherapy of depression.

The Need for a Theory-relevant Description of Depressive Disorders

A well-known excerpt from the Gospel may be useful to illustrate the strategy of the present investigation:

Ἄνθροπός τις κατέβαινεν ἀπὸ Ἰερουσαλήμ εἰς Ἰεριχώ, καὶ λῃσταῖς περιέπεσεν· οἳ καὶ ἐκδύσαντες αὐτόν καὶ πληγὰς ἐπιθέντες ἀπῆλθον ἀφέντες ἡμιθανῆ τυγχάνοντα. κατὰ συγκυρίαν δὲ ἱερεύς τις κατέβαινεν ἐν τῇ ὁδῷ ἐκείνῃ, καὶ ἰδὼν αὐτὸν ἀντιπαρῆλθεν. ὁμοίως δὲ καὶ Λευΐτης γενομένος κατὰ τὸν τόπον, ἐλθὼν καὶ ἰδὼν ἀντιπαρῆλθε. Σαμαρείτης δέ τις ὁδεύων ἦλθε κατ'αὐτόν, καὶ ἰδὼν αὐτὸν ἐσπλαγχνίσθη, καὶ προσηλθὼν κατέδησε τὰ τραύματα αὐτοῦ ἐπιχέων ἔλαιον καὶ οἶνον, ἐπιβάσας δὲ αὐτὸν ἐπὶ τὸν ἴδιον κτῆνος ἤγαγεν αὐτὸν εἰς πανταδοχεῖον καὶ ἐπεμελήθη αὐτοῦ καὶ ἐπὶ τὴν αὔριον ἐξηλθών, ἐκβαλὼν δύο δηνάρια ἔδωκε τῷ πανταδοχεῖ καὶ εἶπεν αὐτῷ ἐπιμελήθητι αὐτοῦ, καὶ ὅ τι ἂν προσδαπανήσῃς, ἐγὼ ἐν τῷ ἐπανέρχεσθαί με ἀποδώσω σοι. [17]

A man was traveling from Jerusalem to Jericho, and he fell into robbers' hands; they, after having both robbed and injured him, went away leaving him half dead. By chance, a priest was traveling along that road, and having seen him he passed over. In a similar way, also a Levite, being on the place, arriving and seeing him passed over. A Samaritan, on the other hand, traveling came near to him, and seeing him got upset, and coming near to him bandaged his injuries, shedding oil and wine on them, and loaded him on his animal, then led him to an inn and took care of him: and the next day, upon leaving the place, drawing out two pieces of silver, he gave them to the innkeeper and said to him: 'take care of him, and should his care cost more than that, I will reimburse you when I come back'.

In this parable, three men meet a person who is in pain and extreme need of help: only one of them stops and offers help, the others simply continue on. Jesus tells his disciples this parable to illustrate the commandment to love our neighbor. Neighborhood is not a geographic, ethnic, linguistic or denomination-specific concept. A fellow human being can be felt as a neighbor only through love, through deep identification processes.

Suffering has always generated an array of differentiated responses in men, religious, philosophical and psychological (see Part I). Emotional participation in it can reach a peak of intensity, and so produce states of emotional turmoil.

Participation can even deprive an individual of the capacity to act rationally. Obviously, it is not possible to cry with a man at the same time as one carries out a surgical procedure on him. Professionalism requires impassibility. The medical profession always implies some degree of emotional detachment from the sick. Only a sufficiently detached mind can identify the problem and implement a correct solution to it.

However, different mental assets are required to establish suitable conditions for various types of human actions. This implies the need for highly differentiated affective and cognitive elaboration of perceived phenomena. And, the practice of psychotherapy–particularly dynamic psychotherapy–also has some unique requirements which sharply differentiate it from somatic medicine, including biologically-based psychiatry.

It is important to note that the therapist's emotional reaction does not equate to a factor of disturbance on this model. The role of empathy is acknowledged in most or all therapeutic approaches. However, in psychoanalytically oriented treatments, the therapist's emotional processes and reactions to the patient's statements both play a unique role in both the establishment of therapeutic alliance and in the processing of counter-transference. They are the engine that fuels the treatment (Winnicott, 1947; Heiman, 1950).

Psychoanalytic treatment requires that the psychoanalyst maintain relatively free access to the emotional side of his experience with the patient. A psychoanalytic psychotherapist is consequently called to an observational and personal stance which is very different from that expected from a biologically oriented psychiatrist. If he can not resonate with the patient (if he does not ἐσπλαγχνίζεται), he cannot effectively help.

The practice of dynamic psychotherapy with depressed patients requires a style of organization and synthesis of knowledge which can retain the full scope of information included in the subject's perception of the patient. It needs to integrate behavioral, cognitive and affective data to an extent not contemplated by descriptive psychopathology.

Descriptive psychopathology requires reflection on concrete behaviors. It withdraws from emotion and personal meaning. It relies on a perceptive approach and aims at subtracting from the perception of human realities their exquisite human character. It can therefore benefit from the use of defenses such as dismantling [18] and de-animation (Mahler, 1968), both of which restrict emotional involvement with the object of observation.

In contrast to this, psychoanalytic psychotherapy assumes that every human fact always implies emotion and meaning. A psychoanalytically informed psychiatrist or psychotherapist needs to honor the full range of emotional depth included in the patient's material. He, too is required to be in touch with concrete behaviors, but he is also required to resonate with the disguised elements of human fantasy life as they underlie the depressive symptoms.

To him, de-animation, dismantling and associated defensive strategies are all obstacles to the perception of a depressive condition. They amount to a distorted mirror, disguising and concealing the patient's bleeding flesh. The psychoanalytic clinician's unique aim is to look at the patient through this mirror, to see and empathetically experience all the pain and sadness that stands behind the observed depressive symptoms.

In the present chapter, we will offer to psychoanalytically trained clinicians a guide to a broader understanding of depressive symptoms. We will illuminate as far as possible the emotions and fantasies of depressed patients as these affect the symptoms of depression or find representation in them. A further aim is to understand whether, and to what extent, characteristic defensive styles, and intra-psychic and interpersonal object relations can be consistently and typically associated with any given symptom of depression.

In what follows, we therefore examine each symptom of depression. We begin by summarizing how each is conceptualized on the biomedical model as well as in the context of various psychotherapeutic approaches to depression. In the case of the latter, we focus particularly on cognitive-behavioral psychotherapy, as it is widely practiced with depressed patients; also, evidence for its efficacy in the treatment of depression draws on an impressive database. Then, we discuss a possible understanding of each symptom within the framework of the psychoanalytic theory of personality.

TOWARDS
A PSYCHOANALYTICALLY ORIENTED UNDERSTANDING
OF DESCRIPTIVE PSYCHOPATHOLOGY OF DEPRESSION

DSM IV-TR includes several diagnostic categories for the classification of disorders on the spectrum of depressive illnesses. For more severe disorders (Major Depressive Disorder and Bipolar Disorder, but also Schizoaffective Disorder), the depressive clinical picture takes the shape of a Major Depressive Episode [19]. This diagnostic label, which dates back to the mid 70s, (Spitzer, Endicott & Robins, 1975) corresponds to explicit and operational diagnostic criteria, in this case, a specified number of symptoms.

Symptoms of a Major Depressive Episode are hierarchically ordered, depressed mood, and loss of interest or pleasure in almost all activities, being ranked the highest. At least one of these two symptoms should be present if a diagnosis of a Major Depressive Episode is to be established. Taken together, the symptoms from the first and the second levels total eight. A minimum of five from that global list is required for a diagnosis of Major Depressive Episode. Symptoms from the second level include alterations in various bodily functions (sleep, appetite and fatigue threshold) and in the levels of psychomotor activity, in addition to pessimistic, self derogatory or death-related ideation and cognitive difficulties.

Let us try to formulate each of the above mentioned symptoms in a language that is independent of the framework of psychopharmacological or behaviorally oriented psychiatry, one accessible and useful to dynamic psychotherapists as well.

Sadness

From the point of view of descriptive psychopathology, *mood depression* represents a disorder of affect. The term 'affect' refers to long lasting emotional states, not connected to specific objects, which can make up the background of an emotional life. It has been included among the symptoms of melancholia since Hippocrates' *Aphorisms* (VI, XXIII), and continuously referred to up to the present day.

Sadness did not elicit great interest among theorists of psychiatry in the nineteenth century. As G. Berrios stated, "For most of nineteenth century, alienists had a preferential interest in the intellectual functions and their disorders: consequently, the semiology of 'affectivity' remained underdeveloped and contributed little to the emerging definitions of mental disease." [20] In twentieth century, Karl Jaspers devoted only a negligible portion of his treatise (1959) to mood alterations in affective psychosis.

For DSM III and IV, the clinical relevance of *sadness* is independent of social norms which dictate the intensity of sadness which is socially acceptable, or identify events which might be reasonably identified as causes of socially acceptable sadness. Sadness is judged worthy of clinical attention according to given standards: a) duration (most of the day and longer than a week), and b) the joint occurrence of the other above mentioned symptoms. Dejection of mood actually represents an elemental psychic event. It is widely used in clinical communication and descriptions of depression by professionals of all backgrounds.

Loss of pleasure

As we have mentioned above, a second symptom, or rather symptom cluster which possesses primary diagnostic value in the DSM-IV formulation, is markedly diminished interest or pleasure in all, or almost all, life activities. This symptom cluster refers to two distinct functional domains in human mental activity: the intensity of will and the ability to feel pleasure. Descriptive psychopathology consistently identifies a distinct symptom for each of the two types of psychological domains: *abulia* and *apathia*.

The German term *Abulie (Gk. Ἀβουλία)* entered into clinical use as early as 1847 [21] and Littré and Robin defined it as an "absence de volonté." [22] Besides being a symptom of several mental diseases (obviously including melancholia) *Abulie* was thought of as an illness per se.

Now, turning to *apathia*, i.e. lack of emotional reactivity to the facts of life, we must mention that a concern for the loss of emotional reactivity can be traced back to early Western history, in fact, as far back as late antiquity, albeit outside the field of medicine.

In discussing the sin of acedia (see above, pp. 25-31), we reported how Evagrius Ponticus, who flourished in the 4th century A.D., participated in the experience of anchoritic life in the desert at the time of its blossoming and how he, a deeply educated cleric, systematized the pathways to spiritual perfection which some generations of ascetics had already been experiencing.

Evagrius Ponticus deemed emotional anesthesia a truly frightful menace to the monk: "Περὶ δὲ τοῦ δαίμονος τοῦ τὴν ψυχὴν ποιοῦντος ἀναισθητεῖν, τὶ δεῖ καὶ λέγειν; ἐγὼ γὰρ δέδοικα καὶ γράφειν περὶ αὐτοῦ..." ("About the demon making the soul unable to feel, what shall I say? I am even afraid of writing about him...").[23] In Evagrius's experience, emotional unresponsiveness would make the monk unable to feel loathing and hate towards τὴν ἁμαρτίαν and lead him to think of "κόλασεως καὶ κρίσεως αἰωνίου ὡς ψιλοῦ ῥήματος" ("of the scourge and eternal punishment as of empty words") [24] thus opening him up to a path to sin.

Several centuries later, the concept of *apathia* entered psycho-pathological thinking. In nineteenth century, Esquirol considered psychical insensitivity as one of the main symptoms of *lypemania*, (Gk. λύπη + μανία), a condition of extreme pathological mournfulness, and his personal version of classical melancholia.[25] The individual experiencing psychical insensitivity would become impassible to any impression, including those caused by positive life events. Loss of interest and lack of affective reactivity were considered symptoms of melancholia by Bucknill and Tuke (1858) as well. In his *La psychologie des sentiments* (1896), Théodule Armand Ribot (1839-1916), coined the term *anhedonia (Gk. ἀν + ἡδονή)*, literally, lack of pleasure), in order to indicate "l'insensibilité au plaisir" which he observed, among other conditions, in patients in severe melancholic states.[26]

Karl Jaspers, author of the fundamental *Allgemeine Psychopathologie* (1959), classified among disorders of "Feelings and states of soul" both *apathia* and the feeling of the lack of feelings. He defined the former as "a lack of feelings," and distinguished it from the "feeling of lack of feelings," which could be observed, among other conditions, in cases of depression. It consisted of a pitiful "Fühlen eines Nichtfühlens" (feeling of not-feeling).[27] He exemplified the phenomenon as follows:

> The sick complain of being unable to experience any joy, any pain. They feel no more affection to their relatives, everything is indifferent to them ... They feel deserted, empty, dead, they have no more joy of living. They complain of lacking any more participation, any interest. [28]

A lack of feelings is also included among the DSM clinical symptoms of a Major Depressive Episode. In fact, according to DSM IV, a depressed patient may be unable to perceive sadness due to deep apathia. In such cases, "the presence of a depressed mood" may "be inferred from the person's facial expression and demeanor."[29]

In DSM's system of categories, a deep loss of reactivity to previously pleasurable events is associated to a peculiar subtype of depression, namely, *Melancholic Depression.* This syndrome, essentially a contemporary version of endogenous depression, is believed by many clinicians to depend more closely on biological alterations in brain function than others.[30]

On cognitive theory of depressive psychopathology, a loss of motivational drives is a consequence of distorted beliefs about the future. Based on previous, repeatedly frustrating experiences, the depressed patient develops unrealistic, pessimistic forebodings about his future. He comes to expect that any attempt he might make at reaching personal, professional, love relationship or other goals will be doomed to failure, and so renounces altogether any hope or wish.[31]

Descriptive psychopathology distinguishes between *abulia* and *apathia* as symptoms referring to different mental functions. From a psychoanalytical perspective, both point to a lack of libidinal investment in objects and relationships. They are different representations of a reduction in motivational processes. The selection between *abulia* and *apathia* seems to reflect the patient's basic defensive strategies and his attitude to experience needs and wishes as either personally motivated or caused by external circumstances.

Loss of interest in life is a phenomenon which is well known to clinicians who practice psychiatry in an outpatient setting. In fact, the depressed patient is nearly always accompanied by someone who blames him for his low level of interest. Still, translating this symptom domain in psychodynamic language is not an easy or straightforward task.

In fact, psychoanalytic understanding of goal directed activities is varied and multifaceted. In Sigmund Freud's view, a man's creative, productive and instinctually satisfying activities may serve multiple defensive functions. On the one hand, many interests mentioned by our patients' spouses/siblings/daughters/mothers would be considered compromise formations [32], since they allow for only limited and inadequate expression to various drives. Within this theoretical framework, hunting, for example, might be conceptualized as a way of representing and controlling troublesome inclinations to aggression, possibly arising in a highly oedipal personality; in contrast, an intense interest in sewing may disguise a blend of narcissistic wishes to restore an idealized self-image and indicate a need to reach a sexualized control over the male.

Other motivationally charged activities could be considered as sublimatory. Freud termed sublimation man's "Fähigkeit, das das ursprünglich sexuelle Ziel gegen ein anderes, nicht mehr sexuelles, aber psychic mit ihm verwandtes, zu vertausche" ("Capacity to exchange the originally sexual goal with another one which is no longer sexual but rather psychically associated to it.").[33] Through sublimation, Freud argues, the repressed energy of libido is refocused onto socially acceptable, and indeed particularly valued, goals, including scientific research. Later, in his acute study of Leonardo da Vinci's personality and artistic work (1910), he expressed the belief that sublimation was a powerful motive underlying artistic creation as well. Undoubtedly, many occupational and vocational activities, in as much as they involve an interest in the arts, or scientific or social knowledge at different levels of competence (from passive concert listening to active professional painting), or a commitment to any sort of philanthropic endeavor, can be interpreted as sublimatory activities form the Freudian perspective.

Freud's pupil, Melanie Klein, pursued these studies still further and connected goal directed activities to more primitive levels of mental functioning. In her *Psychogenesis of manic-depressive states* (1935), she explained that the increase in goal-directed activity, (which characterizes mania), has the function of defending the still immature Ego "from the most overpowering and profound anxiety of all, namely, its dread of internalized persecutors and of the id." [34]

In order to escape from such anxieties over the fate of threatened love objects, the Ego is compelled to "*master and control* all its objects, and the evidence of this effort is its hyperactivity."[35] From a Kleinian perspective, then, activities oriented to specific goals can conceal primitive defense mechanisms. These defense mechanisms aim at alleviating the terror stemming from the dependence on the objects and the awareness of the subject's substantial inability to protect them.

From this point of view, we perceive an inconsistency between descriptive psychopathology and the psychoanalytic understanding of goal directed activities. Psychoanalysis does not assume these to be a perquisite for healthy mental functioning and is alert to the possible distorting effects they may exert on emotional development.

From this perspective, psychoanalysis is in line with a much older tradition. From late antiquity to the Renaissance, interests or activities were judged by virtually all ascetics, east and west, to be forces which disorient the human soul. In the first book of his *Confessiones*,[36] for example, Augustinus Hipponensis commented with evident frankness on the defensive nature of such activities: "Maiorum nugae negotia vocantur."

A parallel stance against drive cathexis of material objects plays a core role in the existential proposals of the Buddha and his followers. The awakened one warned us against excessive involvement with worldly wishes (*cfr.* Gnoli, 2001) and encouraged constant vigilance and the cultivation of a deep level of detachment.

Unfortunately, we cannot assume that depressed patients have achieved the blissful freedom he advocated. The pain they so distinctly experience is a clear evidence of this fact. Rather, psychoanalysis warns us that goal directed activities may very well serve defensive functions. The often inappropriate level of occupational, vocational, alimentary and social activities observed during manic episodes provides sufficient evidence of this. In the following clinical vignette, the same domain, namely, cooking and housekeeping, represented a problem area in both manic and depressive episodes.

> A female patient suffering from bipolar disorder, Mrs. Fortini, received frequent visits at the Community Based Mental Health Center, due to repeated depressive and manic episodes.
>
> During manic episodes, relatives complained of the excessive energy deployed in housekeeping. In addition, the patient's intense engagement in cooking and the consistent pressure on family members to eat the food she prepared in largely exaggerated quantities were the basis for verbal and physical clashes. The latter were frequently followed by hospital admissions.
>
> During depressive phases, the husband invariably blamed her for her apathy. He reported that she stayed in bed all day long. She neglected housekeeping and never cooked for the family.

Wishes can clearly involve defense mechanisms. Their absence in depression cannot obviously mean that anxiety has waned. Suffering is too intense for this to be the case. Rather, we can speculate that, as depression becomes ever more severe, a defensive strategy of a certain kind loses its reparative or protective efficacy. We do not then see a more mature defensive device, but, as far as we now understand this phenomenon, the collapse of a functioning defensive system as a result of inundation.

What, then, are the bases of this breakdown in motivational systems? And, conversely, which unconscious interpersonal and intra-psychic phenomena can be represented by these consummatory behaviors that collapse into depression?

We can hypothesize that mental pain connected to loss events or to the frustration of narcissistic needs commonly generates efforts on the part of the self to produce and perpetuate events of wish satisfaction in the area of narcissism, or in those areas of the patient's life within which his freedom of movement is highest. It so reduces the need to negotiate gratification with the emotionally more relevant objects of his relational field to a minimum.

Typically, such areas may be represented by work, by the body (fasting, fitness, sports) or social image, or by vocational or recreational activities which may be more or less closely linked to social interactions or even to some type of social status (e.g. painting or coin collection). The manic nature of such defenses [37] is obvious: through such operations, the subject tries to reassure a weakened, castrated, damaged self and to remind it of its own abilities, its uniqueness and its value.

The steep decline in gratification-seeking behaviors that is observable in depressed patients may reflect the intensity of frustration in the relationship with the love object. The patient's disappointment following the withdrawal of the object may have been so extreme that the ideal of a good breast which might be found somehow or somewhere, has been lost. The fantasy that sooner or later the patient's efforts and self-mastery will enable him to attract an adequate level of care and personal gratification can no longer be maintained. The patient's renunciation of any further search for gratification in the social world very likely does reflect this deep hopelessness. He has ceased to look for a love object and assumes that love is no longer available to him in any form.

Vegetative Symptoms

DSM-IV criteria for the diagnosis of a Major Depressive Episode list two aspects of this which seem to refer to bodily functions: *alterations in sleep patterns,* and *changes in appetite or eating behaviors.* The authors of DSM-IV assign diagnostic value to changes in these functions in both possible directions. For instance, insomnia contributes to the diagnosis of major depression as much as hypersomnia.

Loss of appetite and insomnia have been recognized as symptoms of depression related psychiatric syndromes since the fourth century B.C.[38] On the other hand, an increase in appetite was a consistent source of concern for Christian ascetics and was identified with the vice of gluttony.[39] Psychomotor retardation and hypersomnia were listed among the characteristics of the vice of acedia.[40]

Contemporary psychiatry has been able to characterize sleep alterations in depression through polysomnography. The single most frequently reported change in sleep patterns is a shortening of the REM sleep delay.[41]

The symptomatic areas we are concerned with in the present section have frequently been termed vegetative, or even biological. The quality of alterations in body or even brain functions has, however, the epistemological status of a metaphor and does not really constitute scientific knowledge. Psychodynamically oriented psychologists and psychiatrists approach these phenomena with a different style of listening. To their ears, other metaphors do echo.

In fact, within Kleinian psychoanalysis, the infant relation to the breast and the nipple amounts to a basic paradigm for the understanding of normal and pathological human relations. On this model, we may reformulate basic questions about loss of appetite in depression as follows: Why is the child not eating? Why is his mouth not avidly suckling the nipple?

Suckling requires strength. The infant sleeps after doing this because its stomach is full, the work of digestion drains its physical resources. Also, its mouth, and cervical spine muscles have worked hard. They have been strained in order to allow the mandible and the mouth to maintain the optimal position for suckling.

Those who suffer from depression do not eat, love, or act. Perhaps under such conditions, strength and the emotional resources required for turning to the object and being able to receive some kind of love are lacking.

However, we cannot exclude the possibility that a drop in oral libido may contain within itself a more specific representational function of the partial object relation to the breast. Mouth and nipple may be unable to meet for several reasons. Winnicott (1947) taught us that, in the mother, hate can arise from many sources. Nipple availability becomes sporadic then and the mother's rhythms are not consistent with the baby's; or still worse, mother's own anxiety and concerns contaminate her child-caring functions. In response to the child's continual needs, her tension and irritability manifest themselves in rigidity and anger. Extending the metaphor, the process may involve the mother's milk taking on unpleasant smells or even including toxic agents (Eigen, 1999).

The infant's withdrawal of his mouth then disguises a refusal to expose itself to the mother's sadistic oral attacks. Patients talking to us about their weight loss, inadequate hunger, may then implicitly blame their failure to thrive emotionally on parental aggression and emotional deprivation.

Let us revisit the question of *sleep.* Here again the experience of child rearing and of living with children has something to teach us. Putting infants to sleep is not an easy task. Mothers and fathers, and, in the past even grandmothers and aunts, often have a hard job before the little eyes close. Depending on the age of the infant or small child, various strategies can be adopted: rocking, rhythmic singing, bodily contact, magic or religious rituals, storytelling.

Clearly, a large number of the tactics employed in putting children to sleep serve the purpose of alleviating separation anxieties, which are so intense at this stage of human life. The content of the anxieties of adult depressed patients is unlikely to be similar to those of an infant, at least in most cases. However, children teach us that sleep onset is a complex and delicate process, one which can take place only in so far as the mind reaches a state of adequate relaxation.

Wilfred R. Bion has described the human mind using the metaphor of the digestive tract.[42] I believe this metaphor can be useful to us in attempting to understand sleep dysfunction as it is associated with depression. The digestive tract is relatively at rest only when both the proximal, gastric portion—which takes up food and carries out a first elaboration of it, and the distal portion—which is devoted to the expulsion of inassimilable residues, are relatively free from food and feces respectively. Given this metaphor, then, the enemies of sleep consist mainly of intense emotional experiences and the defensive operations activated with the aim of containing (i.e. digesting) them.

Painful or anxiety provoking mental content may be avoided through devices which redirect attention to less upsetting issues. From this point of view, financial problems, health issues and occupational risks, are substantially less ominous to the self than distressing conflicts with the love objects. Such issues may easily linger within our depressed patients' mind through the long hours of the night.

We may then speculate that the patient who spends a substantial quantity of psychic energy in order to avoid focusing his attention on painful mental contents is unable to fall asleep. The uninterrupted activity of the mind and the effort of constantly focusing on mental contents that are irrelevant to the most active sources of anxiety at any given time prevent the mental apparatus from achieving a state of relative passivity and drowsiness.

Undoubtedly, such mechanisms co-operate to cause the sleep disorders observed in manic conditions. But, they must play a role also in depressive insomnia, most notably in patients who are presenting with initial insomnia and a clinical picture which reflects a prominent rise in the level of psychomotor activity.

However, the most typical sleep alteration in depressive disorders is terminal insomnia. According to DSM IV, it is a criterion for the diagnosis of melancholic depression, a subgroup of depressive conditions taken to be typical or core syndromes. And, these conditions are thought to have a biological base.[43] Bion's metaphor of the digestive tract may be an aid in understanding this latter type of sleep dysfunction.

In fact, in clinical practice with depressed patients, gastrointestinal system symptoms are often reported.[44] I personally feel the most typical gastrointestinal symptom in depressed patients is constipation. The following clinical example speaks to this.

> Mr. Scuroni had been suffering from a mood disorder since his early adult life. Anamnestic information indicated that the patient and his relatives had sought help chiefly for marital conflicts, which became intolerable when the patient began to blame his wife for extramarital affairs, without material evidence. The patient had retired for some time when I first met him. He attended psychiatric visits at the community based mental health center with his wife and their youngest daughter, who was planning to get married.
>
> In the first period of treatment the clinical picture was dominated by high irritability towards his wife and daughter. Starting with the period immediately preceding the youngest daughter's marriage, aggression towards the wife waned slowly but steadily, and the main focus of the interviews shifted to chronic stipsis, from which the patient was suffering. Frequency of bowel activity showed that such constipation had only a subjective character.
>
> The patient face was now sad and anxious, the flow of his words had became slower, and his sleep was irregular. It was difficult not to interpret the recent transformation of his clinical picture in terms of a swing from a moderate hypomanic condition to one of depression. And of these depressive conditions, constipation was the most upsetting symptom.

From the point of view of the present discussion, I take the temporal relation observed between change in symptoms and changes in family life to be particularly meaningful. Subjective constipation replaced aggression shortly after the patient's daughter had announced she was about to leave the family house and get married. Session contents showed that the resulting painful feelings of loss could not be worked through verbally by the married couple. They remained undigested, unprocessed within the parents' minds and, at a concrete somatic level, within the patient's bowels.

If we now extend this metaphor to the general population of depressed patients, it can offer us valuable hints for understanding sleep alterations in depression. The painful and stinking material lies not in the bowel, then, but rather in the patient's mind, as no adequate resources are there for processing it. Its highly primitive nature is not amenable to the direct action of emotional processing, in Bion's language (1962), of α-function. It cannot therefore find a tolerable representation in dreams. Evacuative mechanisms which the depressed patients have been using on other occasions for expelling such painful contents have lost their efficacy, either because of a generalized traumatic damage to the mind, or because of the decreasing availability of the love object to absorb the patient's massive projection. The mental pain associated with such contents then becomes so upsetting that sleep patterns are affected.

Under such circumstances, sleep is not likely to be brought on by the achievement of a state of rest. Instead, it would be initiated by the exhaustion of nervous system which follows the processing of an excessive load of distressing emotions. Unprocessed, upsetting mental contents would then continue to linger within the self. As soon as the first hours of rest have reduced the biologically based need for sleep within the encephalic structures, memories of painful experiences would resurface and the patient would inevitably wake up early. Hence, the clinical phenomenon of 'terminal insomnia'.

Feelings of Low Self-Esteem

Following DSM-IV criteria for major depression, we now shift our focus from the body to the domain of self-representation. Low self-esteem is a diagnostic criterion for a Major Depressive Episode. DSM-IV underscores the relationship between low-self esteem and guilt feelings and acknowledges that these feelings can reach the level of delusion.

Cognitive psychology interprets the *poor self-image*, with reference to both performance level and ethical standards, as an expression of a distorted perception of one's own image. And, a negative self-image is one of the elements of the triad of evaluation errors which, in Beck's opinion, represent the core elements of depressive syndromes.[45] According to Beck and Weishaar (1989), such distortion would stem from the application to current emotional experience of cognitive schemata which developed during infancy and childhood in connection with traumatic experiences.[46]

Exactly what sort of relation exists between mental pain and self esteem? Psychoanalysis of narcissistic disorders teaches us that low self-esteem is often caused by an inadequate emotional investment in the infant and child by the parental couple (Kohut, 1971). Psychoanalytic theorists often underscore the presence of severe narcissistic injuries in depressed patients.

Freud believed that the narcissistic quality of the object relationships of depressed patients was particularly important. He deemed them substantially incapable of intense and persistent libidinal investment in the objects.[47] Abraham underlined the traumatic role of "Schwere Verletzung des kindlichen Narziß-mus" ("severe injuries to child narcissism")[48] due to " ... zusammentreffende Liebesenttäuschung" ("... cumulative love disappointments"). After World War II, Bibring (1953) and Fenichel (1945) insisted again on narcissistic deficits associated with the difficulties experienced by depressed patients.

Guilt issues which characterize depressive symptomatology have also been the object of investigation by psychoanalytic theorists outside the framework of the study of narcissism. The severity of the problem of Super-ego in depressed patients was stressed by Melanie Klein in *A contribution to the psychogenesis of manic-depressive states.*[49] She referred the phenomenon to the peculiar intensity of the splitting processes in the first stages of development.

However, in spite of the multiple readings of guilt and self-blame issues from the psychoanalytical perspective, the interpretation proposed by the father of psychoanalysis has continued to be the most influential one. Freud conceptualized guilt feelings associated with depression in light of his general theory of object introjection as the core process underlying depression.

He believed that the blame which the depressed patient placed on himself was actually "Vorwürfe gegen ein Liebesobjekt" ("objections addressed to a love object").[50] Through identification with the love object, the blame addressed to the Self displayed, in phenomenal terms, the hostility directed towards the frustrating love-object.

Meta-psychological considerations aside, clinical observation offers us important clues to understanding self-deprecatory feelings as well as guilt feelings in depression. Clinical experience teaches us that these reproaches are not only cases of self-blame: they are often a matter of retaliation, or even aggression, devices directed towards the external object. In interpersonal interaction within family systems, or in the context of the therapeutic relation, criticism to the Self becomes transformed into a device which serves the purpose of ensuring interpersonal control. It often succeeds in setting the object in a position of absolute helplessness; it leads him to the extenuating circumstance and hopeless task of filling in narcissistic deficits, or otherwise compels him to be silent. The framework of guilt can then serve the purpose of expressing within the patient's close relational context or the therapeutic relation, the patient's own sadistic aggression towards his immediate objects. While this aggression, if directly expressed, would elicit immediate or feared retaliations, when it is placed within the context of the language of guilt, it does not precipitate hostile reactions. Instead, it is effective in violently countering the object's narcissism.[51]

The following clinical vignette offers some intriguing insights into the role that guilt and delusion may play within a depressed patient's object relationship system.

Mrs. Luisa Epuloni had been suffering for decades from a severe depressive disorder, associated with obsessive ruminations and pseudo-hallucinations featuring religious themes. She was married to a very slender and fragile man, and was mother of two. A 24 year-old daughter had received a psychological treatment at the Mental Health Community Center where I worked for the emotional sequelae of an attempted rape. Luisa's son was in his teen years at the time.

When I first met the patient (I replaced a colleague who was relocating to a different facility), the clinical picture was characterized by severely depressed mood and guilt ideation. The patient connected her guilt feelings to the religious domain. The moment she received the Holy Communion, fecal phantasies became focused on the sacred Host.

But the guilt ideation followed a different pathway as well, one more closely reflective of the patient's actual relationships. Even in periods when the patients maintained a relative sense of well being, she talked to me at length about her own inadequacy as a mother, especially with regards to her daughter, who in her late childhood had more directly experienced the patient's state of poor emotional responsivity, withdrawal, apathia, and severe chronic depression.

When I first met the patient, her daughter was trying to develop a minimal sense of autonomy towards her family group. Until then, she had been unable to reach a stable professional identity or to establish a love relation which had meaningful potential for the development of an authentic life as a couple. Lengthy portions of our interviews were occupied with the patent's ruminations on her inadequacy as a mother with her daughter's developmental difficulties.

After some years, the symptomatology of the case underwent a sharp change. Her hallucinatory and pseudo-hallucinatory symptoms became massive and widespread, while the usual behavioral inhibition was substituted for by increasing agitation. This led to a significant episode of aggression, at the time hospital admission. After the patient's discharge, symptoms diminished and, over the course of a few months, the clinical picture came to be dominated again by depression and guilt ideation.

Only then did I learn that the daughter had begun occupational training, fostered by the regional administration. Some months had elapsed, and the young woman established herself in a significant love relationship, one which apparently aimed at the progressive construction of the life of a couple outside the parental family.

The patient's suffering was very intense. At this stage, the manifest symptomatology was dominated by depressed mood and pseudo-hallucinatory experiences. Her stomach threatened to punish her for her past wrongdoing, and foretold that she would experience the fate of the rich man in the Gospel narrative (Lc 16, 19-31), who, after living a life of luxury, paid the penalty of his indifference towards the poor and the suffering in hell by being subject to excruciating torments. In fact, in the ultra mundane life, a peculiar exchange of roles had taken place and the poor Lazarus, after having experienced the rich man's self-indulgence for all his earthly life, refused to slake the rich man's thirst on the grounds that the laws of the Hell were inviolable. In the patient's phantasy, her daughter's progress towards the establishment of an adult identity had unsettled the existing power relations within the family. The child and adolescent daughter had lived on the few drops of love that her mother had been able to spare for her. Now, at least in the patient's phantasy, the daughter enjoyed the paradisiacal happiness of autonomy and erotic love, and she would not share a drop of it with her mother. Hell had devolved upon the patient.

Psychomotor Agitation and Retardation

Levels of motor activity are frequently altered in depression. DSM-IV diagnostic criteria for a Major Depressive Episode include psychomotor agitation or retardation. In addition, fatigue or loss of energy are listed as distinct symptoms, though they cover a partly overlapping semantic area. In essence, the contemporary nosography of depression encompasses both an increase in psychomotor activity, ranging from restlessness to overt agitation, and slowing of psychic and motor functions, to both observable behaviors and subjective feelings of exhaustion.

Restlessness and agitation have been included in the description of depressive psychoses since the Hippocratic era (fourth century B. C.). In late Roman civilization, fatigue was included among the features of the dangerous capital sin: acedia (see above, pp. 27-31; see also Azzone 2008).

The nineteenth century French psychiatrist, Ribot, believed that fatigue could be conceptualized as an internal sensation analogous to hunger or loathing. He empirically observed that feelings of fatigue could be focused on different body parts: "Les uns la ressentent [...] dans les muscles; les autres sous forme cérébral. Et voici quelques exemples: «tiraillements musculaires dans les mollets, le dos et les épaules, les yeux gros; mais nulle pesanteur a la teste»; «sensation de relâchement, de fardeau, localisée dans les épaules [...]»; «lenteur aux mouvements, avec sentiments de poids dans la tête»; «lassitude générale, état diffuse; surtout pesanteur dans la tête et fatigue de l'esprit»; «douleurs articulaires et pesanteur cérébrale»." ("Some people feel it (...) in the muscles; the others in a cerebral way. Here you find some examples: «muscular twitchings in the calves of the legs, the back and the shoulders, the eyes swollen; but no heaviness in the head»; «a feeling of relaxation, of a burden, located in the shoulders [...]»; «slowness of movements, with feelings of heaviness in the head»; «general lassitude of a diffuse kind; chiefly heaviness at the head and mental weariness»; «joint pains and a heavy feeling in the brain.»" [52]

Jaspers (1959 [1964]) discussed fatigue in the context of work performance dysfunction.[53] He distinguished objective physical exhaustion from subjective feelings of fatigue.

On the cognitive model of depression "Apathy and low energy may result from the patient's belief that he is doomed to failure in all efforts."[54]

From the psychoanalytic perspective, an increase in psychomotor activity may be interpreted as evidence that the patient's mind is burdened by an excess of emotional experiences. To illustrate this, we draw again on W. R. Bion's psychoanalytically based theory of thought. As we mentioned earlier, in his view, emotional experiences surface within the unconscious mind in the form of raw precursors of thoughts. These he termed ß-elements.[55] ß-elements as such are so emotionally intense that they cannot be usefully employed as components of unconscious fantasies.

In order to become amenable to more elaborate processing procedures, they need to be contained, i.e. worked through, either intra-psychically or interpersonally. Whenever an adequate container is missing, ß-elements persist in an unelaborated form and surface behaviorally as an indeterminate pressure on the motor system. In essence, on a psychoanalytic understanding of depression, an increase in psychomotor activity indicates that a patient's emotional burdens have not been given a sufficient hearing and have not been adequately soothed by the patient's main love-objects.

A patient's psychomotor retardation and fatigue seem to allude to a distinct emotional experience. This parallels a symptom discussed above: the loss of motivational strength. In the introjected object relationship, underlying a decrease in motor activity, the patient's main love object is not merely characterized by withdrawal from him, but rather by injury to him. Efforts at receiving love and nourishment are met by rejection and aggression. In the patient's experience, the longing for satisfaction of emotional needs is consistently associated with the pain of being emotionally hurt.

Descriptive psychopathology has long been aware that fatigue runs parallel with the experience of pain. Bodily fatigue, the pain the astenic depressed patient perceives whenever he tries to set in motion his body, is a possible a representation of this emotional experience.

At the interpersonal level, the depressed patient is hurt whenever he turns to the object for love and care. Where the body is concerned, he feels enhanced fatigue whenever he moves in an attempt to satisfy his needs.

Death Wishes and Suicidal Acts

As far as contemporary researchers in the history of medicine are aware, "hate for life" was first described as a symptom of melancholia by Rufus Ephesius, a physician in imperial Rome.[56] Subsequently, it has been considered a component of all nosographic entities associated with severe depressive symptoms.

Freud's understanding of suicide in the context of depression is embedded in his theory of object introjections.[57]

> das Ich sich nur dann töten kann, wenn es durch die Rückkehr der Objektbesetzung sich selbst wie ein Objekt behandeln kann, wenn es die Feindseligkeit gegen sich richten darf, die einem Objekt gilt, und die die ursprüngliche Reaktion des Ichs gegen Objekte der Außenwelt vertritt.

> the Ego can kill itself only inasmuch as, through the indirect way of the object introjection, it can treat itself as an object, inasmuch as it is able to direct to-

wards itself the hostility which referred to an object, and which substitute the
originary reaction of the Ego against objects of the outer world.

From this perspective, suicide is an act of aggression against the inner object,
against that with which the depressive patient is identified; at the same time,
however, it is an act of aggression against the external love object. In fact, by
killing himself the suicidal patient hurts the breast, the love-object he depends
on for his emotional survival. He hurts it indirectly, by eliciting the infinite pain
of mourning the loss of a loved one.

In *Trauer und Melancholie* (1917), Freud does not explicitly pose a question that is implied in his theoretical formulation of suicide: Which factor
blocks a more direct course of action in a depressed patient? Which factor for-
bids him to concretely kill the love-object, as sometimes tragically happens in
conditions of psychosis or drug dependence?

Some clues to the understanding of these issues come from a later work[58] in
which Freud proposed a different formulation of the phenomenon of suicide. He
there developed the hypothesis that the suicidal patient would be identified with
the goals of a particularly severe Super-ego, and so would come to be the per-
former of the death sentence which an extremely harsh conscience has pro-
nounced upon the Ego.

In fact, in clinical practice depressed patients show a profound difficulty in
expressing aggression towards the love-objects upon whom they depend. If,
consistent with Freud's theory[59] the Super ego is constructed through the introjection of parental figures, then we can understand that the suicidal patient is
used to a lived relational experience with objects which are extremely severe
and judgmental about any form of opposition to them. The terror that such interpersonal violence is able to generate permanently inhibits any form of hostility that may be expressed directly. In such a context, the aggression or murder of
himself represents to the patient the only possible strategy for hurting the object, albeit in an obviously indirect way. The anger and hostility elicited by frustration can find expression only by orienting themselves against what Freud
called the *introjected object*.

The Kleinian approach contains elements which may further contribute to
the understanding of the forces which affect the direction and the object of aggressive acts. From the point of view of Kleinian theory of human development,
two different configurations of defenses, anxieties and characteristic fantasies
are activated sequentially. These are called schizo-paranoid and depressive positions (1952).

In the schizo-paranoid position, prevailing in the first fourth months of life
and associated to psychotic syndromes, predominant anxieties refer to the objects' aggression toward the self. The subject feels he is immersed in a hostile
environment, and continuously in danger. In the paranoid position and in related
clinical conditions, aggression is fantasized and acted out in the relation between the self and the object.

The depressive position is associated, in Melanie Klein's view (1935), with melancholic states, and according to her followers, with both normal development and neurotic states.[60] Anxieties focus on the fate of the object. The subject perceives the risk which his own aggression poses to the object and desperately attempts to repair the damages he has caused.

When compared with Freud's views, the Kleinian perspective seems to lead to an opposite understanding of the dynamics of suicide in depression. According to Freud, it involves directing aggression towards the self in order to implement an admittedly costly and indirect attack on the love object. In contrast to this, Klein's theory of depressive position would have us conclude that the depressive patient commits suicide in order to preserve the object.

Can we possibly advance the hypothesis that the choice to act out hatred through a definitive attack on the self stems from such needs for protection of the object? That the suicidal act represents an extreme attempt at sheltering the object from aggression which cannot otherwise be restrained?

In my practice, one of the aspects which uniquely characterizes interpersonal relations of depressed patients is their intense dependence on aggressive love-objects who display high levels of interpersonal power. Experience seems then to suggest that fear and the expectation of the objects' retaliation are the factors which marshal the depressed patient's powers of aggression and force him to turn it against the self. It is not the concern for the object which stops him, but rather the ontogenetically primeval fear of punishment.

In the following clinical vignette, psychodynamic observation illuminates the relation between suicidal impulses and interpersonal interactions.

Mrs. Bruna's *Weltanschauung* was explicitly inspired by the values of dependency. Apparently, the marked positive quality that contemporary society lends to autonomy in both affective and professional life left her unmoved. She naively stated she was in the constant need of the presence and care offered by her daughter, her two sons and her husband.

When her daughter decided to get married, the patient manifested a depressive episode characterized by dejected mood, feelings of desperation, extreme fatigue, severe appetite and weight loss and multiple somatic complaints. The requests for constant presence and care she formulated to her relatives became more and more frequent and exasperating, and any frustration of them elicited childish and theatrical behaviors.

After having been admitted to internal medicine divisions of hospitals a number of times, the patient was referred to the psychiatric ward. In spite of several psychopharmacological treatments, her mood became increasingly worse, particularly after the daughter got married. The exhausted relatives, in turn, came to increasingly reject the patient. Both her daughter and the patient's husband insisted on her permanent placement in a psychiatric community. In this social context, the patient began to indulge in phantasies of putting an end to her life by leaping out the window.

I met the patient for the first time after she had twice attempted to act out such phantasies. In fact, her relatives had been able to control her attempts without much difficulty. I asked her to explain the situation to me. She told me of the plan of final expulsion from the family as it had been conceived by her relatives.

For her part, she had unhesitatingly agreed with it. She told me she was determined to live no longer without the constant and permanent assistance of other human beings. Apparently, she was not as much concerned whether such a task was to be carried out by her relatives, or by the more anonymous social or mental health workers. Moreover, she was fully aware that her sons', daughter's and husband's resources were completely exhausted.

The patient's manifest statements expressed absolute compliance with her relatives' deliberations. Towards them I recorded no criticism, no anger. However, clinical observation seemed to suggest that her unconscious experience was quite different.

While talking about her urge to throw herself out of the window, an urge she felt unable to resist even then, she repeatedly brought her hand to her mouth, and then moved it forward. That gesture reminded me of an effort to vomit. I felt that, in the patient's mind, her husband's and daughter's refusal to offer her the care she needed was equated with her expulsion from the family group, in the same way our bodies expel, through vomit, the nutrients that cannot be absorbed in the digestive tract.

In the patient's fantasy, her body was thrown, or was in danger to be thrown, out of the window in order to meet its final destruction; similarly, she felt she had been eliminated forever from her family's core.

Cognitive Difficulties and Problems with Concentration

Cognitive difficulties and problems of concentration are not included in the Hippocratic description of melancholia, nor are they reported in the classical works of Rufus, Galen or Ishaq Ibn Imran which treat of such illness (Jackson, 1986). Hence, if we are to identify a pre-modern description of the cognitive difficulties associated with feelings of sadness and discouragement, then we must search for them outside the field of medicine. These kinds of phenomena are mentioned for the first time by an ascetic: Evagrius Ponticus (see above, pp. 30-31).

The difficulties that the monk has to struggle with in the course of his journey, Evagrius called demons. In subsequent centuries, they came to be known as mortal sins. Among them was the particularly malicious demon of acedia. Its features included difficulty in concentrating, restlessness and sleepiness. Evagrius did not explicitly associate acedia with the sin of sadness, which he conceptualized as a distinct and dangerous obstacle on the monk's path of personal purification. But since Gregorius Magnus's *Moralia in Job*[61], *tristitia* and *acedia* had come to be considered an expression of a single sin, though it encompassed sadness, abulia, apathia and difficulty in concentrating.[62] And, this association was to persist through the centuries of the Middle Ages.

Physicians' interest in the cognitive features of melancholia is undoubtedly more recent. Cognitive performance deficits more commonly detected in depressive syndromes are described by traditional psychopathology in terms of states of inhibition. Kraepelin[63] included the dearth of ideas among the symptoms of depressive episodes of manic-depressive psychoses. In his *Allgemeine Psychopathologie* (1959), Karl Jaspers described this class of phenomena among the complex deficits of performance of the human mind, and specifically among the anomalies in the unfolding of the psychic life. Jaspers contrasted inhibition of thought to the flight of ideas observed in manic states, and interpreted the former in terms of the reduction of associative processes and of loss of the power to actively direct cognitive processes by the representation of the goal.[64]

As can be seen, in traditional psychopathology, attentional and concentration deficits are considered an expression of a basically quantitative deficit of an ideational activity, conceived as an ability to spontaneously and continuously produce contents. From this perspective, then, depressed patients' difficulties in cognitive performance would express a *quantitative* reduction in the activity of the mind, rather than an alteration of the principles regulating its functioning. Only in most extreme forms of cognitive deficits, as these are associated with depressive states, did psychiatrists of the nineteenth and the first half of the twentieth centuries focus their attention on *qualitative* dysfunction in the cognitive processes.

Specifically, alienists of the nineteenth century, beginning with Esquirol (1838), termed such syndromes (whose etiological status remained very unclear for a long time) *vesanic* dementias; the concept of '*melancholic* dementia' entered into general use at the turn of the same century. The term pseudodementia has been used only since the 1950s [65] to indicate the (reversible) poor cognitive performance observable in the course of some psychoses.

Aaron Beck was the first psychiatrist to fully appreciate the importance of cognitive difficulties which can be observed in a wide population of depressed patients, and the first to demonstrate how, in addition to those forms of general and severe cognitive debilitation which can be observed only in a minority of cases, more subtle cognitive deficits are practically ubiquitous in depressive states.

According to Beck (cfr. Beck and Weishaar, 1989) and his school of thought in cognitive psychotherapy, a relevant etiological or at least pathogenetic role should be conceded to these cognitive deficits. From this perspective, most or even all symptoms of depressive disorders can be traced back to cognitive deficits. Consequently, those cognitive symptoms which are commonly included in psychiatric clinical descriptions of depression could as well.

In fact, the cognitive distortions described by Beck and his co-workers represent subtler dysfunctions of the cognitive processes. They are not detected by a traditional mental examination, and consist of peculiar styles of interpretation of life events and understandings of one's own identity. With reference to the ability to think or concentrate, or to cognitive performance more generally understood, distortions mentioned by cognitive psychotherapy theorists appear to be causative factors.

Particularly, with reference to difficulties in thinking or concentrating, Beck and his co-workers [66] believe that these can be explained by the hypertrophy of negative schemata which characterize depressive patients. When such schemata become too pervasive, the patient is unable to detach from them and focus on new contents of perception connected to realistic activities, and so he is not able to set his or her sights on any definite goals.

On the other hand, a difficulty in making decisions can be explained in terms of the patient's inability to realistically appreciate the consequences of the differing behavioral options available to him. "Often the patient will not make *any* decisions because of the negative results he foresees." [67]

Let us now consider this from the psychoanalytic perspective. Within this framework, thought processes have been studied chiefly in terms of patterns of organization and the working through of experience. The capacity to establish a tie between emotional processes and informative contents has been deemed a particularly important core factor. An important basic contribution to this was the work of Wilfred Ruprecht Bion (1962).

We have already mentioned Bion's theory of thought in the context of our discussion of the phenomena of psychomotor agitation and retardation as these are manifest in depressive symptomatology. Descriptive psychopathology has basically conceptualized those cognitive deficits which are clinically detectable in depressive states in terms of phenomena of ideational-inhibition, i.e. in terms of the cognitive equivalents of retardation of motor activity. An analogy between motor and cognitive deficits is clearly consistent with the unique metaphoric style of Bion's thought. It invites an extension of the application of Bion's theory of thinking to the problem of understanding the cognitive deficits associated with depression.

From this perspective, when the emotional climate gets darker, mental resources are dramatically diminished. Particularly, when the subject is the focus of an acute interpersonal aggression, when he is subject to massive projective identifications from love-objects, these repeated painful experiences overwhelm his ability to work through mental content and so limit his powers of self-transformation.

The mind then receives an overflows of β-elements, i.e., of traumatic experiences lacking a dream-like representation, or of precursors of such experiences (Bion 1962). Their impact on the psychic apparatus may be compared with that of toxic gas (Eigen, 1999).

Under these conditions, anxiety and pain lack any ideational representation. Still, they surface in so far as they impact upon cognitive processes. Attention cannot be properly focused on the cognitive tasks of everyday life as, at some level, the subject perceives the presence of more pressing and distressing contents somewhere in the self.

On the other hand, an undefined sense of fatigue is perceived in association with any effort at thinking, as the working through of the underlying anxiety and pain consumes a large portion of the patient's stamina for processing mental content. Our depressed patient's complaint about his inability to think or concentrate may well be the phenomenological consequence of a collapse of the capacity for thinking and processing emotional information.

THE CLINICAL IMPACT
OF A PSYCHOANALYTICAL CONCEPTUALIZATION
OF DEPRESSIVE SYMPTOMATOLOGY

The paradigm we rely on for interpreting experience significantly affects the range and direction of clinical investigation. In the present chapter, we have compared the psychopathological and psychoanalytical points of view as they are applied to depressive symptomatology. The objects of investigation of descriptive psychopathology are events of human life. It describes them in terms of the functions of personality, or of the mind. Since it is is the offspring of the philosophy of faculties [68] and, in some way, a more developed and concrete form of eighteenth century phrenology, descriptive psychopathology dissects the emotional experience of human life and reduce it to an array of functions (attention, memory, perception, ideation, psychomotor activity, affect) which reflects those studied by neurophysiology and neuropsychology. It defines the study of emotional experience on a template drawn from the study of brain functions and of the effects of traumatic, vascular, degenerative, neoplastic or inflammatory lesions on the central nervous system.

A man lies in bed for a long time. An intense anxiety about the future of his marriage torments him and he is unable to sleep. Descriptive psychopathology would formulate this situation as a sleep disorder. As concerns the insomnia reported by the patient, it clearly does not negate or exclude altogether the possible etiological role of life events experienced by the human being in the vignette. It might be classified as a situational insomnia. It is obvious, however, that the articulation of scientific knowledge produced by the psychopathological approach will foster research strategies focusing on physio-pathological sleep mechanisms.

On the other hand, classifying our patient's condition as a problem typically associated with marital couples might connect it to more or less typical difficulties associated with transition in the life cycle. And, this second perspective is very likely to foster research interests and therapeutic interventions which are very different from the former ones.

We have here reviewed the symptoms of depression as they are conceptualized by descriptive psychopathology. Specifically, we have tried to trace each of these formulations of elemental events, segmented and reduced to basic functions of the mental apparatus, back to human experience. And, with the term 'experiences' we refer to complex representations of interpersonal events organized around motivational forces; to multiple self and object perceptions arising in the course of reciprocal interactions; and to processes of cognitive elaboration of perceptions and the affective responses stemming from them. We have also attempted to trace cerebral functions (such as memory, sleep-wake and eating rhythms and so on) back to fusion wishes, fears of being controlled, jealousy and feelings of powerlessness. From a general perspective, I believe that this translation process has shown how, also in cases of severe depressive suffering which clinicians encounter everyday in their practice, it is possible to look behind the concreteness of symptoms and see the forms of a series of human meaningful experiences.

This approach allows the clinician to address the problems of the patient suffering from depression in a new fashion. He can orient his listening toward the emotional difficulties of a fellow human being, to his personal history, his interpersonal context, his suffering. He can benefit from an awareness of the elements which his own personal suffering has in common with the patient's. And, he can work out his own interventions on the basis of a realistic appreciation of the emotional forces and of the objects (see Arieti, 1977) which dominate the patient's life.

Behind a lack of libidinal or oral wishes, he can also observe a chronic frustration experience; behind a psychotic agitation, the overflow which inhibits the normal functioning of the mental apparatus; behind enhanced appetites, the effort to actively control painful feelings. Guilt feelings and even guilt delusions then reveal and represent the inadequate affective investment the patient is perceiving from his love-objects: insomnia can be evidence of interpersonal aggression within the patient's immediate family.

Where do these reflections lead? Can we now consider treating depressive patients without the support offered by traditional psychopathological descriptions? Can we safely state that psychopathology is the product of a particular observational stance, modeled on the paradigm of somatic medicine, described in Chapter 4? It seems not.

Epidemiology shows us that certain configurations of emotional events (which descriptive psychopathology calls symptoms) commonly co-occur in subjects whose mood is depressed. The history of medicine teaches us that such configurations have been observed and reported by clinicians in a consistent manner for over two thousand years. Medical anthropology (Kleinman and Good, 1985) has shown that analogous clinical pictures are detectable in many cultures others than the Western one, although the shape and focus of the patient's complaints may vary.

We have already shown that the depressive syndrome develops at the interface between two subjective experiences, that of the patient and that of the physician. We might say the same of the symptoms of a depressive episode. Depressed mood, insomnia, anorexia, the wish to die are emotional realities: they are actually experienced as such by the patient and observed by the clinician.

For centuries, depressive illness and its symptoms have been, and may forever be, perceived as an apt and useful representation of the emotionally painful conditions by both the suffering human beings and those who seek to help them. Thus, both patient and physician represent pain in terms of symptoms of an illness, in terms of functions and dysfunctions of mind and body.

Emotional experience is painful. It is undoubtedly painful to the physician, who, as noted above, fears an inundation of emotions which would make his professional functioning impossible. But, the free communication of emotional experience would be just as much painful to the patient, who is frightened by the possibility that aggression might pollute his relation with his love-objects; and humiliated by both the width of his own dependency on them and the weakness associated with the narcissistic investment of his love objects in him. This is why he chooses to overvalue, in the context of his own experience of pain, concrete, bodily elements (I eat/I do not eat, I sleep/I do not sleep), *versus* the emotional ones (my beloved does not love me, my beloved does not listen to me), the facets of experience he thinks he can control (I am bad, I want to kill me) *versus* the areas where he more clearly perceives his powerlessness (my beloved does not appreciate me, or does not care for my life or, even, for him/her I might as well be dead), the role of functional performance (I can't work, my motivational forces left me) *versus* the nature of intimate relationship (the people I love flood me with their projections and make me collapse).

The therapeutic encounter between patient and physician or psychotherapist elicits an intensification of the pre-existing mental pain already implied by depressive states. The special constellation of defenses, fantasies and character traits which underlies manifest depressive symptoms serves to alleviate such suffering and enables the patient to draw the attention of the interpersonal field to his own suffering. For narcissistically injured, basically alexythymic (Honkalampi et al., 2000), pained patients, depressive symptoms represent core strategies for communicating intense, albeit disguised, experiences of emotional pain and establishing a potentially helpful external object relationship.

Within such framework, depressive symptoms can be conceptualized as a network of representations of experiences and communicative devices which aim at the containment of mental pain. However boring or irritating might they be to the therapist, they are somewhat mitigated forms of projectively identifying onto the therapist emotional events which cannot be perceived without experiencing pain.

Depressive symptoms are the basic content of the therapist's perceptive activity during the therapeutic encounters. Through them, though in very refined or disguised terms, the patient's painful experiences are communicated to the therapist's mind. The therapist can develop empathic insight into the patient's emotional world only as far as he can be receptive to these events and is willing to emotionally process them within the framework of a network of projective and introjective identifications.

Depressive symptoms are extremely valuable components of the communication between the depressed patient and his therapist and, at the same time, of their real and imaginary relationship. However, they can serve such a purpose only in so far as the therapist does not treat them with the same distancing procedures that are operative in the patient's mind; inasmuch as the therapist is able to process them in a manner which makes it possible for them to retain their human, live and emotionally original quality.

It is my hope that translation of the symptoms of depression from psychopathological terms, into the language of conscious and unconscious emotions and relations, as it is here proposed, can aid in this.

NOTES

1. Gabbard, 1990 [1992], p. 168.
2. Karasu, 1990b, p. 273.
3. Ibidem, pp. 274-275.
4. Ibidem, p. 276.
5. Einleitung, p. 284, ll 5-6.
6. Ibidem, ll 14-19.
7. *Kritik*, Elementarlehre, 1. Theil, Trans. Aesth., p. 50, ll 4-5; "The undetermined object of an empirical intuition is called «phenomenon».
8. *Kritik,* Elementlehre. I Theil. Transcendentale Ästhetik, p. 50, ll. 6-14
9. *Kritik,* I. Abschnitt, Von der Raume, p. 55, ll. 2-5 & 9-11.
10. *Kritik*, II. Abschnitt, Von der Zeit, p. 59, ll 19-23 & 31-32.
11. *Kritik,* II. Abschnitt. Allgemeine Anmerkungen, p. 65, ll. 9-21.
12. Ludwig, 1975, p. 603.
13. Ibidem, p. 604.
14. Engel, 1977, p. 130.
15. Ibidem, p. 132.
16. Nineteenth century astronomers discovered that various observers would invariably attach slightly differing values to the same phenomenon. This systematic bias was termed 'the observer's personal equation.' (Schaffer, 1988)
17. Lc 10: 28-35.
18. Meltzer et al., 1975, p. 21.
19. APA, 2000a, pp. 349-365.
20. Berrios, 1996, p. 289.
21. Berrios, 1996, p. 362.
22. Littré & Robin, 1855, p. 7.
23. *De malignis cogitationibus*, 11, 1-3.
24. Ibidem, 11, 7-8.
25. Esquirol, 1828, pp. 398-481.
26. Ribot, 1896, p. 84.
27. Jaspers, 1959 [1964], p. 120.
28. Ibidem.
29. APA, 2000a, p. 349.
30. APA, 2000a, pp. 419-420.
31. Beck et al., 1979, p. 12.
32. From his work of 1896 onward (see p. 387), Freud conceptualized symptoms of obsessive neurosis as a compromise between the forces of the wish striving for satisfaction and those repressive forces elicited by the subject's anxieties. Later, he extended this perspective to most, if not all, symptoms and generally to all products of the unconscious mind. (see 1916-1917, p. 373)
33. Freud, 1907, p. 150.
34. Klein, 1935, p. 277.
35. Ibidem.
36. I, IX, 15.
37. Klein 1935, pp. 277-279.
38. Hippocrates, *Epidemiae*, III, XVI cases; case 2.

39. Evagrius, *Practicos,* Chs. 17-18.
40. Evagrius, *De octo spiritibus malitiae*, col. 1159B.
41. Akiskal, 1995, p. 1130.
42. Bion, 1975 [1991], pp. 3-5.
43. APA, 2000a, p. 419-420.
44. Gorad, et al., 1996, Ladep et al., 2006.
45. Beck et al., 1979, p. 11.
46. *Cfr.* also Beck et al., 1979, p. 16.
47. Freud, 1917, p. 435-436.
48. Abraham, 1924, p. 147.
49. Klein, 1935, p. 267-268.
50. Freud, 1917, p. 434.
51. Freud, 1917, p. 438.
52. Ribot, 1896, p. 147.
53. p. 224.
54. Beck et al., 1979, p.12.
55. Bion, 1962, pp. 6-7.
56. Ruphus Ephesius, *Fragmenta*, p. 355.
57. Freud, 1917, p. 439.
58. Freud, 1923, p. 283.
59. Freud, 1923, p. 262.
60. Hinshelwood, 1993, Ital. ed., p. 82.
61. Vol. 76, coll. 620-622.
62. Jackson, 1986, pp. 65-77.
63. Kraepelin, 1902, p. 283.
64. Jaspers, pp. 227-230, Ital. ed.
65. Berrios, 1996, p.190.
66. Beck et al., 1979, p. 13.
67. Ibidem, p. 186.
68. Berrios, 1996, p. 17-19.

Chapter Five
Encountering Depression in the Context of Mental Health Services:
The Contribution from Psychoanalytic Literature

The most useful books tend to draw on direct clinical experiences, on the immediate encounter with patients. Whenever clinical experiences reveal parallels to those we ourselves have met in our practice, proposed theoretical formulations and clinical recommendations are likely to gain our consensus, or otherwise illuminate features of work we either have performed or will be carrying out in the near future.

In the present chapter, we review psychoanalytic literature on depression. It is actually a limited amount of material, especially where the high prevalence of depression in contemporary society is concerned, but also as to its position at the core of prevailing psychiatric nosographies. From available contributions, we have selected those which have apparently had a deeper impact on subsequent authors. However, we have not attempted to outline an historical picture of the great authors of the past, neither to trace the lines of theory development in an effort to somehow represent the debate within the psychoanalytic movement, nor have we reviewed other theoretical paradigms of psychotherapy. Instead, we rely on personal criteria in organizing the discussion here. We have tried to highlight those theoretical formulations which displayed more extended parallels with the patients whom we or our close colleagues meet every day in clinical practice.

The observations collected here are consistently heavily influenced by features of my practice and they are drawn from that setting. The clinical experiences which I drew upon in writing this chapter were had, for the most part, in a psychiatric outpatient facility. They include both psychoanalytically oriented psychotherapies and dynamic psychiatric treatments. I place a high value on the information obtained from dynamic psychiatric patients as it gave me access to a very large number of different clinical pictures and conditions of intra-psychic and interpersonal interaction.

It is my hope that, in spite of this limitation, the present review of clinical formulations of depression be of some help to readers, be they psychiatrists, clinical psychologists or psychotherapists. Or, perhaps the direct relation to personal practice will make it excessively idiosyncratic? It is impossible to answer this question at this point, but I think that these pages may be useful to readers in so far as they will depend on shared experiences. I believe that clinicians who work in direct contact with depressed patients in their everyday practice, and who have emotional experiences in a field similar to the author's may be able to find here resources of interest and convergent points of view. They may also be challenged to develop constructive reflections from a dialectical perspective.

THE LOST OBJECT

Our journey starts with the work of the father of psychoanalysis. Sigmund Freud turned to the study of depression only after his interest had been elicited in it by a contribution of a brilliant pupil, Karl Abraham. But, this aside, no one can deny that *Trauer und Melancholie* (1917) exerted a massive influence on all subsequent psychoanalytic literature on the subject. Freud's ideas about the genesis of depressive experience were straightforward:

> In einer Reihe von Fällen ist es offenbar, daß auch sie [*i.e.* melancholia] Reaktion auf den Verlust eines geliebten Objekts sein kann; bei anderen Veranlassungen kann man erkennen, daß der Verlust von mehr ideeller natur ist. [...] So würde uns nähe gelegt, die Melancholie irgendwie auf einem dem Bewußtsein entzogenen Objektsverlust zu beziehen, zum Unterschied von der Trauer, bei welcher nichts an dem Verluste unbewußt ist (1917, pp. 430-431)

> From a series of cases, it is obvious that it [i.e. melancholia], too, can be a reaction to the loss of a loved object, in other circumstances it can be ascertained that the loss is of a more ideal nature [...] So, we are inclined to believe that melancholia should somehow be connected to the loss of an object, a loss subtracted to awareness, unlike mourning, in which nothing of the loss of the object remains unconscious.

Contemporary psychiatry no longer gives much weight to the classical distinction between reactive and endogenous depression. On the other hand, psychiatrists working in the field still place a value on the absence of substantial and perceivable stressful life events when they are first assessing an episode of depression. They focus their keenest attention on those patients who state they have not undergone adverse experiences and prescribe for them not only the most specific medications, but also more structured psychological treatments.

Freud's hypothesis that this subgroup of patients has actually suffered from the loss of a love object, albeit "von mehr ideeller nature" ("of a more ideal type") can be assessed in clinical practice. In my personal experience, the onset or recurrence of a depressive syndrome is very often associated with deep changes in the network of relationships in which the patient is immersed. Often, though not always, they are the result of his or her having arrived at a new stage of the life cycle.

CLINICAL VIGNETTE NO. 1. For some years, Mrs. Natalina Onestini had been receiving help at our Community Mental Health Center for an obsessive compulsive disorder. She was a woman in her sixties, perceivably overweight. She was the mother of a married daughter and the grandmother of a female child. The relationship with her daughter appeared to be defined by intense expectations of receiving love and care from her - expectations which the daughter had largely left disappointed. A moderate coolness has resulted among the two of them; it was a source of pain to the patient. A short time before the onset of the obsessive symptoms, the patient's daughter had decided to introduce her small child into a kindergarten. Until the age of three, the child had been cared for by the patient most of the day.

Moderate doses of fluvoxamine promoted substantial improvement in the patient. After a sustained period of full remission, I agreed with the patient to terminate follow-up. At the same time, I assured her of my availability in the case of future needs.

Six months later, the patient's husband told me that her clinical condition had deteriorated again. The clinical picture was no longer dominated by obsessive symptoms, but by dejected mood, severe aboulia and anhedonia. Her husband had to fully care for the patient and take care of the housekeeping. At the same time, a compulsion had appeared, one never previously noted: Every day the patient checked hundreds of times whether the pajama trousers that she wore all day long had a hole in the perineal area.

Neither the patient, nor her husband had any hypothesis as to the causes of this recurrent behavior. An increase in the doses of serotoninergic medication produced no benefits, the therapeutic relationship deteriorated steadily and the patient became less and less available to meet with me. In a clinical interview, the patient's husband reported to me incidentally that, at the time, his wife was unable to help their daughter, who was again pregnant.

Any attempt on my part to discuss the relationships between the various family members in the interviews proved inconsequential as the patient and her husband put up massive resistance. The same was true of any effort to involve the daughter in the treatment program. A couple of hospital stays also had no appreciable effect on the patient's condition. Only two months after her daughter delivered her baby, did the patient begin to show some evidence of improvement. It increased over the following months.

In this clinical example, the object mourned for, even though it had been denied by the patient and her relatives, was identifiable by the treating psychiatrist within the domain of the patient's relationship to her daughter. The changes that the new pregnancy prompted within the family network seemed to be central to the genesis of the new episode of illness. In the following clinical vignette, the separation anxieties experienced within the therapeutic relationship played a core role.

CLINICAL VIGNETTE NO. 2. Mrs. Mastrulli was a very short, middle aged woman who looked at the interviewer with unusually intense eyes. Her personal history was very sad, but not uncommon among patients at psychiatric facilities. She was the daughter of a single mother, spent her childhood in an orphanage, and joined her mother only in adolescence. She herself was the mother of two little children, the elder of whom was at the time entering primary school. Her husband's intellectual resources were minimal but his devotion to the patient was unquestionable.

I met the patient in the emergency room when she was experiencing an outburst of anxiety and weeping. She was decidedly restrained about her interpersonal problems. A number of interviews at the community mental health center enabled me to superficially explore the vicissitudes of her painful childhood. Pharmacological treatment was followed by substantial improvement in her symptoms.

I had been meeting the patient periodically on a flexible schedule for a year or so, when she experienced a recurrence of the depressive symptoms. At the time, she explicitly requested the support of a psychologist. I could not understand her request against the background of our rather irregular relationship and referred her to a female psychologist.

This colleague formulated a time-limited, focused treatment plan. Some months later when I met her, she communicated to me that the psychological treatment had come to end as planned. Shortly thereafter the patient experienced another, still more severe episode of mental illness. The symptoms now included depressed mood, thoughts of death, abulia and fatigue. Anti-depressive medication produced only limited benefits.

The patient's husband was now expected to bear an intense emotional burden. He assisted his wife through a number of hospital admissions, and took over the larger share of the child care and housekeeping responsibilities. At times, he appeared hopeless.

I naively proposed to the patient's psychotherapist that she resume treatment, but she showed no willingness to consider this option. A patient's symptom seemed however suggestive of an intense unresolved erotized transference toward a female object: whenever she saw a plastic bag she was caught by an irresistible longing to put her head in it. Only through her own and her husband efforts she was able to resist.

In the latter case, as in the former, the onset or the worsening of depressive psychopathology was traceable back to the patient's emotional and relational history. Unfortunately, clinical practice shows that this is not always possible. In many instances, prolonged observation does not enable the clinician to identify the concretely or symbolically lost object. Ought we to suppose, as Freud actually did (1917, p. 440), that this substantial minority of depressed patients in outpatient practice expresses a biologically based, genuinely endogenous disorder? Or, ought we rather to focus on the patient's and even the therapist's defense mechanisms?

To the therapist, achieving an adequate awareness of the patient's interpersonal relationships and the affects connected to them implies a complex process. It can fail due to a particularly rigid defense mechanism in the mind of the patient, but also due to hostile feelings towards the therapist or the use of manipulative strategies towards him. In a parallel fashion, although the clinician relies on empathy in order to understand the patient's experience, the identificatory processes are highly liable to distortions as they are promoted by the emotional interactions experienced in the relationship with the patient. The following clinical example illustrates such dynamics.

> CLINICAL VIGNETTE NO. 3. Emergency situations had been a prominent feature of Mrs. Matilde Cislaghi's mental disorder since its onset. Vague somatic complaints and anxiety brought her to our hospital Emergency Room repeatedly in search of help. Engaging the patient in a community mental health treatment program turned out to be an arduous task. In the morning, she met me in the Community Mental Health Center. Her husband or one of her sons always participated in the interviews. In the afternoon, she sought help at the Emergency Room, the next morning from the head of the psychiatric department. The next afternoon I met her at the outpatient facility.
>
> The interviews were always brief. The patient seemed unable to tolerate any communication with me for more than few seconds. She was able to express her severe depressive feelings only at the prompting of her relatives. However, she never got beneath the surface: dejected mood, loss of any interest or pleasure in life, severe anergy. The fear or rather terror elicited by the prospect of a minimally meaningful contact with a psychiatrist may have been related to the excruciating loss of a son, who had drowned himself three years earlier.
>
> These interviews with the patient and her relatives allowed me to understand that medical and psychiatric visits were happening only to pressure from her relatives. The patient had no other wish than to deepen her dependence on her husband and, to a lesser degree, on the surviving sons and a sister-in-law. Given such an interpersonal scenario, medical visits were experienced as acts of retaliation by her relatives in response to her endless craving for care.
>
> Her intolerance of the treating psychiatrist came to be reflected in an intolerance to the varied drug treatments (neuroleptics, benzodiazepine, SSRI) which either I or other psychiatrists had prescribed for her. My hesitation to empathize with the patient's intense oral avidity, the severity of her mechanisms of denial, and the primitive level of her thought processes undoubtedly hindered my understanding of the pain which had unsettled her life in an apparently unforeseen fashion. However I believe that my availability to interact with her relatives and my implicit alliance with some punitive and recriminatory components of their relationship to the patient played a decisive role in making any form of genuine communication between her and me substantially unachievable.

As mentioned, Freud, too, acknowledged that he was in many cases unable to identify or bring to light the object loss which he had hypothesizes as the underlying cause of depression.

SADISM

> Die unzweifelhaft genußreiche Selbstquälerei der Melancholie bedeutet ganz wie das entsprechende Phänomen der Zwangsneurose die Befriedigung von sadistischen und Haßtendenzen, … [1]

> The undoubtedly delightful self-tormenting of melancholia, just like the corresponding phenomenon of obsessive neurosis, means the gratification of sadistic and hate tendencies…

Psychiatrists know too well the feeling of annoyance often elicited by depressed patients, especially in chronic cases and those who are resistant to treatment. And, the people who are closest to the sick person and who are with him at the time of the visit are those who are most clearly annoyed. The patient is blamed with sloth, emotional greed and, above all, inconsistent motivation to improve. What were Freud's views on this subject?

> … pflegt es den Kranken noch zu gelingen, auf dem Umwege über die Selbstbestrafung Rache an der ursprünglichen Objekten zu nehmen und ihre Lieben durch Vermittlung des Krankseins zu quälen, nachdem sie sich in die Krankheit begeben haben, um ihnen ihre Feindseligkeit nicht direkt zeigen zu müssen. [2]

> … in addition affected people are usually able—through the indirect pathway of self-punishment— to take their revenge on originary objects, and to torment their close relatives with their state of illness, a state into which they have recoiled in order to avoid being compelled to directly express their hostility towards them.

In Freud's view, some symptoms of melancholia actually are helpful to the sick person as instruments for tormenting the people who are close to him. Through it is outwardly addressed to the self, aggression actually becomes directed at the introjected object. Renouncing food, drink, and emotional exchange, the sick person withdraws from the important shared emotional experiences of his love objects. Hesitating to improve, he withdraws from the treating clinician narcissistic rewards within the professional domain.

In fact, as early as 1912, Karl Abraham had reported enhanced aggression in melancholic patients.

> In den uns hier beschäftigenden Psychosen verbirgt sich ein anderer Konflikt. Er nimmt seinen Ausgang von einer überwiegenden Haßeinstellung der Libido, die sich zuerst den nächsten Angehörigen gegenüber geltend macht, sich dann aber verallgemeinert.[3]

In psychoses which concern us here, is another conflict concealed. It moves from a prevailing hateful tendency of libido, which initially let itself be evident toward the closest relatives, but then get generalised.

We may ask ourselves, then, why the patient should harbor such intense aggression feelings towards individuals who make an effort to aid in the patient's well being. Freud formulated the following hypothesis:

> Die Person, welche die Gefühlsstörung des Kranken hervorgerufen, nach welcher sein Kranksein orientiert ist, ist doch gewöhnlich in der nächsten Umgebung des Kranken zu finden. [4]

> The person who has elicited the emotional disorder of the sick person, to which his state of illness is oriented, is, however, commonly to be found in the patient's closest relations

Everyday psychiatric practice can only rarely provide support for such an hypothesis. Commonly, fatigue, loss of pleasure or of emotional reactivity primarily upset existential and libidic adjustments of the objects basically available to the patient, those at least partially willing to help him. In the relational configuration associated with the depressive disease, this position is often occupied by the patient's sexual partner in adulthood, and by a son or daughter in old age.

When a "love disappointment," in Freud's language, i.e. the actual or symbolized experience of abandonment from a love object is actually to be observed, aggressive or sadistic strategies by the depressed patient do not seem able to effectively reach out to the frustrating object. In the first clinical vignette cited here, there is good evidence that Mrs. Onestini's emotional breakdown had been provoked by her daughter's faltering emotional availability. But the preferred victim of her sadistic attacks was her husband. Apparently, the sick's person's rage becomes exacerbated just because the most cherished object has been able to place himself outside the scope of the patient's clutch, safe and far away.

THE DEPRESSIVE POSITION

According to Melanie Klein:

> ... wherever a state of depression exists, be it in the normal, the neurotic, in manic-depressives or in mixed cases, there is always in it this specific grouping of anxieties, distressed feelings and different varieties of these defences, which I have described and called the depressive position.[5]

Klein described typical anxieties in this mode of functioning as follows:

> As the ego becomes more fully organized, the internalized imagos will approximate more closely to reality and the ego will identify itself more fully with

'good' objects. The dread of persecution, which was at first felt on the Ego's account, now relates to the good object as well and from now on preservation of the good object is regarded as synonymous with the survival of the ego. [...] this situation, namely, when the ego becomes fully identified with its good internalized objects, and at the same time becomes aware of its own incapacity to protect and preserve them against the internalized persecuting objects and the id. This anxiety is psychologically justified.[6]

Melanie Klein had been more recently charged with not having been able to properly differentiate the depressive position from clinical depression.[7] Actually, the Viennese born psychoanalyst believed that the defense mechanisms observed in depressive psychosis "play their part in the *normal* working-through of the infantile depressive position."[8] For purposes of the present discussion, however, we wish to understand whether the identification of typical psychological devices which characterize the depressive position can be of any help, or whether they could in any way be observed within clinical practice with depressed patients.

In fact, when melancholic patients are observed in a traditional psychiatric setting an enhanced concern on their part for the well-being of their love-objects is not immediately perceptible. They undoubtedly express severe guilt feelings of varying degrees of intensity towards partners, parents, and children, but such feelings apparently lack any power to limit aggression and sadism, and, as noted, it is these features of their condition that so commonly infiltrate the object relations of melancholic patients.

However, we can gain a wider perspective on this issue if we expand upon the limited information available through observation of individual patients and supplement it with a thorough anamnestic investigation of the relationships with those objects which are actually invested with a particular parental or libidic value. The selfish requests for care and the extreme unavailability to collaborate in any mutually gratifying activity at once dissolves, then makes room for a singular attitude of compliance. The aloofness towards objects disappears and what is then revealed is a tenacious and indissoluable connection to the object. The following clinical vignette clearly exemplifies these dynamics:

CLINICAL VIGNETTE NO. 4: I have been treating Mr. Alfredo Cesariano for about 5 years on a thrice, then twice weekly basis. This was done in a psychoanalytic psychotherapy setting. After about 4 years of treatment, the patient was emerging from a dissociative episode, one which had lasted 3 weeks and required a neuroleptic treatment. Having regained sufficient mastery over his own emotional life, he began to display increasing feelings of dissatisfaction with his precarious occupational situation, loss of interest in life activities, fatigue, decrease in appetite, a decline in libido, and low self-esteem. The depressive syndrome lasted for about 9 months.

The acute psychotic crisis had developed at a time when the patient had become close to a female neighbor. Their relationship continued marginally over the next few months, then slowly dissolved altogether.

The patient suffered from sentimental difficulties, but to him the most intense source of pain was his mother's icy attitude toward him. She lived in a large city in Northern Europe and typically got in touch with him only once every three to four months.

The mother's emotional withdrawal elicited in the patient a strong wish for retaliation. The latter found expression in a level of hostility and detachment fully resembling that of his mother.

Mr. Cesariano did not write, nor did he telephone her. He also never visited her. However, the therapeutic work allowed me to detect better and better a precise correlation between events in the relationship with the mother and shifts in the patient's mood.

Any occasional contact with her (postcards, messages on the automatic responders, birthday greetings) was invariably followed by weeks of depression, ideational and psychomotor retardation, as well as poor work performance. And, the diminishing frequency of meetings with the mother did not weaken the negative impact that this relationship had exerted on every facet of the patient's emotional life. On the contrary, it further enhanced his sensitivity to rejection and the painful longing to experience once again the warm and affectionate availability which she had at times shown to him during his childhood.

We don't know whether these separation issues, albeit often skillfully disguised by massive levels of denial, reflect those intense introjective mechanisms which, in Klein's view, arise from the severe anxiety over the fate of the love-object. For the Viennese psychoanalyst, such anxieties give rise to "a child's exaggerated fixation to its mother or whoever looks after it"[9], but in clinical practice with depression the wish "of making reparation to the object" [10] which, according to Klein, is the most specific evidence of the depressive position, cannot be clearly detected.

ORAL AND ANAL DRIVES

At the end of last section we mentioned the oral introjective mechanisms which Klein deemed essential for the working through of the depressive position. Her mentor, Karl Abraham, had been the first psychoanalyst to point out the presence of intense oral needs in melancholic patients:

> Vertiefte Einblicke in die Struktur der depressiven Psychosen haben mich zu der Annahme geführt, daß bei den Kranken *die Libido auf das primitivste uns bekannte Stadium ihrer Entwicklung regrediere*, auf jenes Stadium, welches wir als das orale oder kannibalistische bezeichnen lernten.[11]

> Thorough investigations into the structure of depressive psychoses led me to the belief that in the patient's *libido regresses to the earliest stage of development which is known to us*, to the stage which we have learnt to indicate as oral or cannibalistic.

In a subsequent contribution, Abraham explained the phenomenon of object introjection (which Freud had identified as the core process of depressive psychopathology in his *Trauer und Melancholie*, 1917). He construed it in terms of oral incorporation:

> die Introjektion des Liebesobjektes ist, wie ausführlich nachgewiesen werden soll, ein Vorgang der Einverleibung, wie er einer Regression der libido zur kannibalischen Stufe entspricht [12]

> introjection of love object is, as it shall be widely shown, a process of incorporation, as it corresponds to a regression of libido to the cannibalistic stage

In the same context, however, Karl Abraham felt the need to reformulate his theory of drive fixation in melancholia. In the wider framework of a general revision of Freud's theory of psychosexual development, Abraham reconceptualized the depressive regression to the oral stage as the final step in a regressive process, one which began at more mature developmental stages. According to this new formulation, the melancholic patient's psychical organization would then be initially characterized by a sadistic-anal fixation. Functioning in this mode, the patient would activate mechanisms of expulsion and destruction of object relationships. This would unavoidably push him to regress to sadistic-oral levels of functioning.[13]

Traditional clinical descriptions of depressive syndromes include some elements which can be associated with specific problems within anal and oral areas. Appetite loss or enhancement are factors in the diagnosis of depression, while conflicts with respect to control and expulsion are evidenced by the possible co-occurence of obsessive symptoms or syndromes; alterations of digestive and excretory functions, particularly in older patients, are also considered to be evidence of this (*see* above, pp. 70-71).

Can these clinical phenomena offer adequate evidence of specific drive related issues? First of all, where oral drives are concerned, can we safely state that, in depressive conditions, a stronger incorporative wish is observed than in other psychiatric syndromes? Or, a more intense or poorly controlled longing for care and emotional gratifications? Or, does the need for control of affects and relations prevail, a need which can, at times of more severe crises, result in a tendency to reject the object? Such questions lead us to the general issue of the relation between affective syndromes and specific personality traits. It is one which dates back at least to Kraepelin (1901) and is still the focus of theoretical and clinical discussion (Kernberg, 1988) and empirical investigation.[14]

From a general perspective, a specific level of personality organization (according to Kernberg, 1984) cannot be identified among depressed patients. In clinical practice, depressive syndromes can be observed among neurotic, borderline and psychotic patients. In my experience, and roughly parallel to this, many different specific personality configurations, descriptively defined, may develop depressive symptoms: narcissistic, schizotypal, borderline hysterical, obsessive personalities and others.

The wide range of modes of personality organization notwithstanding, to whatever extent they evidence severe but varying difficulties in the area of Super-Ego rigidity, levels of psychosexual development, defense mechanisms, ego strength, and integration of identity, enhanced dependency upon the object is a very common and perhaps even ubiquitous factor in clinical depression. Clinical vignettes 1 and 2 above demonstrated how the withdrawal of emotional nourishment and care can elicit extremely intense experiences of pain, experiences which come to be expressed as the classical symptoms of depression. In the following clinical vignette, a long-lasting oral frustration came to be associated with a neurotic level depressive syndrome:

CLINICAL VIGNETTE NO. 5: When I first met Mr. Piercarlo Trovato he was a trade-agent in his forties. He was married to a very active woman and was proud to be able to provide for all financial needs of his family. When his only daughter approached the completion of high school, he began to withdraw his commitment to the job and ended up resigning from it.

The consequent deterioration in his financial condition came to torment him. He became dejected, pessimistic and apathetic. His symptoms lasted about two months and then he responded well to a treatment with a serotoninergic medication. He was easily able to find a new employment in a different branch of the trade.

A year and a half later his daughter became engaged. Around the same time, Mr. Trovato decided to open a business of his own. To this end he contracted a substantial debt and did so without sharing any of this information with his wife. Some months later, he realized his business was developing much more slowly than expected and revealed to his wife the full extent of his financial obligations. Financial problems were again the focus of a somewhat realistic ideation of ruin. His commitment to work declined, and his guilt feelings increased.

His wife, a highly determined, very realistic and, at times, hypo-manic woman, brought him to me twice for psychiatric consultation. She was deeply annoyed with her husband. Need had compelled her to find a job and she angrily reported how her husband had abdicated his role as the basic support of the family.

Manifest guilt feelings notwithstanding, the interview revealed that Mr. Tovato was at least as angry with his wife as she was with him. The discussions made it clear that he had consistently chosen the very business options which were likely to bring about the financial disaster. At the same time, illness prevented him from making up for it.

Only through my prompting did he get to give limited expression to his anger towards his wife for the increasing coldness and annoyance she had been showing toward him. Mr. Trovato stuck to his defense of his idealized image of the wife, and repeatedly underlined that any frustration she had administered to him should be considered as an unavoidable and justified reaction to his unreliability and poor productivity. But, he could hardly keep back tears when he reported that their shared times had been reduced to few minutes at the beginning and the end of the day.

When I mentioned that the possible marriage of the single daughter might weaken the family's financial situation in the near future, Mrs. Trovato was clearly moved. Tacitly, I formulated the hypothesis that Mr. Trovato couldn't tolerate the cooling and affective withdrawal of his wife, her retreat into herself in this difficult transitional phase in the life-cycle.

The case of Mr. Cesariano (CLINICAL VIGNETTE n. 4, above) clearly revealed an intense need for gratification of dependency needs as they are commonly observed in clinical practice with depressed patients. It demonstrated the enhanced persistence of such emotional ties. In less severely disordered patients, highly dependent relationships to love-objects generally appear less obviously pathological. Still, they are very much essential to the patient's emotional survival and understanding them can be very arduous, particularly given that such patients are subject to massive levels of denial.

From this point of view, clinical material undoubtedly confirms the hypothesis proposed by Abraham in 1916, though certainly not the extended theory formulated in 1924. While aggression and sadism are constantly observed in the melancholic's object relationships, I don't believe the expulsion drives that Abraham located in the first step of anal-sadistic stage ("expelling and destroying") correspond to the tenacious quality of dependency relationships. The latter survive through severe withdrawal and even savage acts of aggression on the part of the object.

NARCISSISM

The belief that narcissistic issues and problems play a substantial role in the etiology of depression or in depressed patients' character organization is widespread in psychoanalytical literature. Karl Abraham believed that a "Schwere Verletzung des Kindlichen Narzißmus durch zusammentreffende Liebesenttäuschungen" ("severe damage to child narcissism through cumulated love disappointments") [15] was a key factor in the subsequent development of a melancholic syndrome.

Freud focused his attention on the peculiar object relationships he was able to observe at the time of symptom onset. He believed that:

> ... die Objektwahl auf narzißtischer Grundlage erfolgt sei, so daß die Objektbesetzung, wenn sich Schwierigkeiten gegen sie erheben, auf den Narzißmus regredieren kann. Die narzißtische Identifizierung mit dem Objekt wird dann zum Ersatz der Liebesbesetzung, was den Erfolg hat, daß die Liebesbeziehung trotz des Konflikts mit der geliebten Person nicht aufgegeben werden muß. Ein solcher Ersatz der Objektliebe durch Identifizierung ist ein für die narzißtischen Affektionen bedeutsamer Mechanismus; [16]

... the object choice has relied on narcissistic bases, so that the object cathexis, when it is confronted with difficulties, can regress to narcissism. The narcissistic identification with the object becomes then a substitute for love cathexis which has the consequence that the love relation, the conflict with the loved person notwithstanding, has not to be abandoned. Such a substitution of the object love through identification is one quite important mechanisms producing narcissism-based disorders

Consequently:

Die Melancholie entlehnt also einen Teil ihrer Charaktere der Trauer, den anderen Teil dem Vorgang der Regression von der narzißtischen Objektwahl zum Narzißmus.[17]

Melancholia owes a component of his character to mourning, the other one to the process of regression from the narcissistic object choice to narcissism

A narcissistic object choice is, in Freud's view, an object choice which aims at satisfying the Self's narcissistic needs. He clearly exemplified this in the following excerpt:

Solche Frauen lieben, streng genommen, nur sich selbst mit ähnlicher Intensität, wie der Mann sie Liebt. Ihr Bedürfnis geht auch nicht dahin zu lieben, sondern geliebt zu werden, und sie lassen sich den Mann gefallen, welcher diese Bedingung erfüllt. [18]

Such women love, *stricto sensu*, with the intensity with which men love them only themselves. In fact, their needs lead them not to love, rather to be loved, and they let themselves give in to the man who satisfies this condition.

Depressed patients' narcissistic problems have been the focus of continuing attention on the part of subsequent psychoanalytic theories as well. In 1945, Fenichel underlined the presence of severe self-esteem deficits in depressive syndromes; and, in 1953, Bibring showed the pathogenetic role of narcissistic wishes as they are fueled by a particularly severe Super-Ego, and the consequent intense feelings of helplessness. More recently, Lax (1989) observed that in personalities displaying a marked narcissistic investment of pathological character traits "Intersystemic tensions between the Ego and the Ego ideal (aspect of the Super-ego) and intrasystemic tensions within the Ego..." give rise to depressive conditions characterized by "feelings of shame and humiliation, rather than guilt." [19] The author termed "narcissistic depressions" such conditions. At the turn of the century, Biancosini et al. (2000) underscored the usefulness of psychoanalytical models of narcissism when they are applied to the problem of understanding depressive pathology.

The complexity of the clinical theory of narcissism and the extreme richness of the clinical phenomena which have been interpreted in terms of narcissistic issues (narcissistic defenses, such as omnipotence, idealization and devaluation, specific object relationship styles, featuring manipulation and insensitivity to object's needs, reliance on ancillary objects serving the function of self-objects, Super-ego pathology, sadism and masochism in object relationships and in sexuality, distortions or damages to the self-image, etc.) compel us to keep our discussion within certain limits. We will therefore review only two components of narcissistic issues as they can be observed in depression-related clinical phenomena: object relationships and the sense of self.

As for object-relationships observed in depressive conditions, the multifaceted relevant clinical configurations cannot easily be summarized. Splitting mechanisms and the wide range of reciprocal identifications contemporaneously enacted with reference to different roles played out with respect to life-cycle stages explain the co-existence of object relations widely differing in terms of the warmth, intensity, reciprocity which the one and same subject can experience in various relational contexts.

However, I would argue that the complexity inherent in the material can be reduced by conceptualizing differing relations according to the axis of care and dependence. From this point of view, independently of the roles socially or traditionally assigned to each family member, we can distinguish relationships in which the subject plays mainly a caring role (according to 'maternal code', Fornari, 1981) from those in which the subject is mainly the object of care ('child code,' Fornari).[20]

Towards dependent objects, children, and more commonly, sexual partners, the melancholic undoubtedly shows a distressing fierceness. Clinical practice almost constantly reveals that husbands or wives are engaged in exhausting caretaking tasks which often involve the complete substitution of the patient in any function relevant to the social role (including working for or earning the family's living, housekeeping, child rearing, *cfr.* CLINICAL VIGNETTE NO. 1). Undoubtedly, poor sensitivity to the object's needs, sadism, and omnipotent control, give these object relationships a manifestly narcissistic character.

The relationship to objects invested with expectations of parental care gives rise to a more complex configuration. Bibring's (1953, p.108) description of feeling of helplessness much more clearly characterizes this second class of interactions. At this level, object relationships clinically observed in depression show no evidence of the weakness Freud described in 1917 (p. 108). Rather, the emotional greed mentioned above with regard to dependency objects here appears to be associated with an extraordinary tenaciousness.

This, in turn, places the melancholic in an extremely vulnerable position. The overwhelming need for emotional care causes him to lose any stamina or capacity for retaliation against the love object. The depressed patient's heroic faithfulness condemns him to defeat. At this very level, the weak components of narcissistic organization—enhanced vulnerability, poor self-esteem, and feelings of inferiority—become obvious in the clinical setting.

Relationships that are strongly rooted in sadism versus masochism, omnipotence versus impotence, and care functions versus dependence are easily perceptible in the clinical vignettes reported above, although only a single pole is often obvious in each case, at least within the limits of observation in an outpatient psychiatric setting. Mrs. Natalini, for instance, demonstrates an unrelenting interest in control and insensitivity towards her husband, while Mr. Trovato displays submission and acute fear of separation from his wife.

Melancholic patients' sense of Self pathology is available for clinical observation in a much easier and more direct way than are object relation dysfunctions. Clinical descriptions of melancholia traditionally include a deeply deteriorated self-image. Self contempt can either take on the titanic proportions of a nihilistic delusion or restrict itself to everyday dissatisfaction with one's own intellectual or professional skills, It is nevertheless ubiquitous in the clinical picture. With reference to traditional descriptions of depression, current outpatient practice may differ only in so far as guilt issues are less pervasive. Interpersonal or social role dysfunctions are more often thought of as the consequence of pathological processes that are independent of the patient's will or caused by insensitivity or unavailability of social or family context.

With reference to the possible etiological role that damage to the Self image may play in the onset of depressive episodes, we believe that "narcissistic depression" constitutes a specific minority within the spectrum of a wider clinical population. In the following clinical vignette, a deterioration in social role functions had a substantial, negative impact on the course of an illness. In addition, for a long time, severe anxieties relevant to self-image prevented the patient from sharing with me essential components of her life.

CLINICAL VIGNETTE NO. 6: I met Mrs. Marianna Sirianni for the first time after a short hospital stay. It had been prompted by a suicide attempt. Mrs. Sirianni told me she had been found unconscious in her flat by her sister, who had become alarmed when she did not answer her phone. The patient was naked and completely wet. Beside her were a few empty packages of benzodiazepines. She was unable to explain me the events of the previous night. She was however aware she had wished to die, a wish that was somewhat still alive within her.

She believed life had no more significance for her. A few months earlier, due to the careless driving of a female friend she had been involved in a car accident and suffered a fracture of the neck of the humerus. The situation had had an unfavorable outcome. Mobility had been severely limited in her right arm, and she had lost the ability to properly make use of her right hand. For several months, interviews with the patient were dominated by her complaints about her disability.

The patient had always been very proud of her effectiveness and commitment to her job and she believed that her employer would never accept her back in this altered condition. She would be only a functionally limited worker. To make matters worse, for the patient's self-esteem her self-sufficiency in taking care of her home had been equally as important. After her parents' death, she had always lived on her own and independence and autonomy had come to be core values to her. Now the fracture of her arm compelled her to rely on the help of a sister in order to handle many home tasks. That hurt her deeply.

Some months had to pass before I came to know something of the patient's emotional life. She progressively revealed to me that, for some time, she had been experiencing a situation of embarrassment. Her heart was divided between two men. The first one lived in Venice with his mother. The patient had hoped to establish a deep tie with him and possibly start living together. But, the man's mother's hostility had caused the plan to fail even before the suicide attempt. At the same time, she had been attached to a married man who spent some months each year in Lombardy on business. This latter tie was much more longstanding than the former one, but since its inception, it had excluded any potential for establishing an authentic life as a couple.

Over the course of the treatment, the patient became steadily aware that there was no realistic chance for a future life together with the unmarried lover and definitively left him. By that time, her depression symptoms had substantially diminished. Against this background, we were able to agree on termination of treatment after a year and a half.

REVIEW OF MAIN THEMES AND CLINICAL APPLICATIONS

We have here reported and reviewed basic texts from psychoanalytic literature on depression. We have compared clinical theories with everyday experience in clinical practice with depressed patients and are now in a position to highlight certain issues which we deem essential, i.e. those which can possibly impact on the general attitude and technique suitable for the handling of depressive disorders within the framework of psychiatric and psychotherapeutic practice.

1. Depressive suffering expresses, and often conceals, the pain of the loss of an object, of a relationship particularly precious to the Self (as underscored recently also by Lopez & Zorzi, 1990, p. 92). The awareness of this connection compels us to reserve adequate room in the collection of anamnestic information for an accurate (to the extent that the patient's personality organization allows) investigation of the patient's real relationships. The various roles played out with reference to the partner, to parents, to sons and daughters, to objects invested with competitive values in various familial and occupational contexts, all need to be explored and assessed. Any actual or potential change within such configurations should be thoroughly explored as it may be a possible factor in either the onset or deterioration of depressive symptoms.

2. Depressive patients typically show a marked greed for attention in interpersonal relationships. Melancholic patients' relatives often point out to us that that emotional and existential resources available to the patient are more than adequate for the average needs of a human being. Indeed, patients themselves very often share this view. However, psychoanalytically oriented literature teaches us that depressed patients' needs for emotional care, attention and narcissistic gratifications are particularly intense. When we encounter a patient who belongs to this diagnostic spectrum, we had best forget the renunciations that we, as human beings, are everyday called to undergo, and try to objectively appreciate the patient's real emotional

needs. We may be surprised to discover that, with reference to the patient's precarious personality organization, the emotional resources made available to him in the context of his interpersonal milieu are dramatically poor.

3.   The melancholic patient is full of anger and aggression towards all human beings, and sadism is to him an important source of gratification. Experience has taught us that the depressive patient's cooperation in treatment is always partial and often discontinuous. Even if the patient is motivated to participate in the treatment, from the perspective of the more mature functioning layers of the personality, at some level one can always detect a wish to hinder those processes that aim at re-establishing well being, as this well being is conceptualized by relatives and mental health system values. This frequently evidences itself in e.g. limited compliance with drug treatments or with the outpatient follow-up schedule. The melancholic can hardly genuinely share treatment goals. His unwillingness to please the people close to him in terms of libidic gratifications and to sustain his share of family duties and responsibilities is to him a very important way of expressing his aggressive drives towards the objects. It will therefore be very difficult for clinicians to establish a satisfactory therapeutic alliance with the patient without an adequate and emphatic understanding of the unconscious goals that are concealed behind symptoms. On the contrary, any effort at exerting pressure on the patient to make him comply with the treatment needs and goals, as they are commonly conceptualized in terms of symptom improvement, entails a great risk. It can lead to the repetition of dysfunctional patterns within the therapeutic relationship. At the very moment, the clinician requires from the patient that he give up his slothfulness and passive aggression, he is showing him the way toward, and giving him the opportunity for, new sadistic gratifications which can be elicited from resistance to the therapist's omnipotent therapeutic strategies.

4.   In depressive syndromes, severe narcissistic deficits are commonly observed, both in terms of object relationships and of sense of Self pathology. Narcissistic problems in the area of object relationships are associated with the distinctive greed mentioned above, and they are the basis for the depressed patient's personality's unique liability to any changes in its network of interpersonal, family and erotic relationships. The very presence of such primitive needs in depressive conditions explains the dramatic impact of separation events. This has been recorded in psychoanalytic literature (see above). On the other hand, a proper awareness of a depressive sense of self-frailty enables us to understand the depressed patient's inability to speak genuinely about his own personality, his core relationships and the roots of his depression. Speaking about oneself often means meeting the dread that the bad, bleak parasitic part of his personality will be perceived by the interviewer, thus irreparably damaging the good, constructive, ethical image of himself, which he desperately needs to build or defend. From this point of view, hiding, or better, *denying* such facts comes to be a vital defence mechanism. Furthermore, this narcissistic liability is the basis for

the severe pathogenic effect which may be produced by life events which variously affect the patient's Self image. In the previous sections we mentioned the features of the depressive configuration which Lax termed "narcissistic depression." We recommend that the clinician attempt to fully appreciate the impact of multiple change events (retirement, growing up of children, job changes, social status improvement or deterioration) on the patient's Self-image.

NOTES

1. Freud, 1917, p. 438.
2. Ibidem.
3. Abraham, 1912, p. 152.
4. Freud, 1917, p. 438.
5. Klein, 1935, p. 276.
6. Ibid, p. 264-265.
7. Hinshelwood, 1993 [1994], p. 82.
8. Klein, 1935, p. 289, my italics.
9. Klein, 1935, p. 302.
10. Ibidem, p. 265.
11. Abraham, 1916, p.108.
12. Abraham, 1924, p. 115.
13. Ibid, p. 117-126.
14. Phillips et al. 1998; Böker et al., 2000.
15. Abraham, 1924, p. 147.
16. Freud, 1917, p. 435-436.
17. Ibid, p. 437.
18. Freud, 1914, p. 155.
19. Lax, 1989, p. 88.
20. *cfr.* Maggiolini 1988, pp. 64-65.

Part III
The Model

Chapter Six
A Model of the Process of Formation of Depressive Symptoms

We have traversed the entire field of clinical depression and explored the history of this disease and its interpretative theories. We have disentangled the threads of its apparently intrinsic connection to brain function, examined its symptoms in depth and shown how some of them may conceal a wide range of human emotions and tears of sorrow. We have also shown how some of these symptoms can fruitfully be conceptualized in terms of modes of functioning of the unconscious mind. Finally, we have reviewed classical psychoanalytic contributions to the understanding of depression and have returned from our journey with a rich harvest of information, insights and strategies for interpreting clinical phenomena.

Now we may possess the elements of knowledge which allow us to assemble a comprehensive picture, to construe the full spectrum of the clinical phenomena of depression in terms of events and processes taking place in the unconscious human mind, i.e. to construe depression as a *psychoanalytic problem.*

In the present, we will therefore attempt to draw up a comprehensive psychoanalytical model of the genesis of the psychopathology of depression. We will start from the experience of pain in the real life, specifically in interpersonal interactions, and illustrate the sequence of psychical phenomena which mental pain can elicit. Lastly, we will show how these basic psychic mechanisms can generate the manifest symptoms of depression.

In developing this model we will rely on no unexplained somatic factors. We will explore only interpersonal and intra-psychic psychological phenomena as these are conceptualized in psychoanalytic theory and applied to psychiatric pathology.

SOURCES OF MENTAL PAIN

Social Attitudes Towards Emotionally Painful Experiences

The sources of human mental pain are many. Sigmund Freud connected clinical depression to the loss of a love object,[1] including losses of a moral nature. Psychoanalytic authors have added damage to the self-image to the list of common causes of depressive states (Bibring, 1953). In fact, empirical research has repeatedly shown that the experience of stressful life events increases the risk of one's developing major depression.[2]

In certain life situations, mental pain is socially perceived as a psychophysiological reaction to negative events or interpersonal configurations. Grief is commonly referred to as the prototype of socially accepted pain related phenomena. The peculiarity of this class of emotional reactions to pain is that they are accompanied by a certain amount of identification and sharing on the part of close family and social relations.

DSM-IV nosography has dropped from its lists a number of the dichotomies previously included on the spectrum of depression. These were widely agreed upon in the first half of last century. A case in point is the dichotomy between reactive and endogenous depression which also disappeared from DSMs.[3] However, even now, the detection of a significant gap between the intensity of the manifestations of the mental pain and the socially perceived severity of a stressful life event distinctively elicits enhanced clinical attention. In my experience, practicing clinicians also still assign great value to such a gap in identifying patients who are particularly in need of structured psychological or pharmacological treatments.

In human societies, some experiences of pain are shared and culturally perceived as acceptable representations of emotional suffering. Others are taken to be incorrect, to improperly represent an individual's emotional life. This incorrectness is differently conceptualized in different societies and certain categories of guilt, demonic possession, systematic error, have prevailed in various historical periods (cfr. Part I). However, the paradigm of illness is surely included among the acceptable categories and depression is the nosographic category currently accepted worldwide for classifying painful feelings which are deemed incorrect.

Of course, the intensity of the mental pain that accompanies depression is a core feature of depressive symptomatology. In fact, the experience of very intense physical or psychical pain in a fellow human being is particularly hard to bear. That may be one reason why we are sometimes unable to maintain an adequate level of identification and empathy, and an explanation for the pressure that it put on people to consequently distance themselves from it by denying the authenticity or correctness of the pain experience itself (*cfr.* above, pp. 19-21).

However, another obviously massive obstacle to the recognition of pain in others stems from the area of narcissistic organization of the suffering individual himself. For many years, psychoanalytic investigation has recognized that intense depressive experiences are often caused by feelings of extreme helplessness and powerlessness (Bibring, 1953, *cfr.* above, p. 97-99). In such situations, the subject's ability to communicate the interpersonal isolation which he is experiencing is severely limited by the feeling that perceiving or communicating his own lack of worth in interpersonal relations would imply a further injury to an already precarious self-image.

For instance, a middle-aged woman who is dominated by feelings of intense jealousy toward her sister-in-law can be totally unable to communicate to herself or others her basic feeling of not having been sufficiently loved by her mother, a feeling associated with absolutely unbearable suffering.

The culture of a given society has a significant influence on the selection of experiences which are allowed to be communicated and reflected upon (*cfr.* Moscovici, 2001; more specifically, Kleinman & Good, 1985). Jealousy in heterosexual relationships is an accepted source of sadness in Western culture. People can talk about it and feel understood by others. Jealousy in the relationship with a son or daughter is, however, generally stigmatized. Clinical experience has shown me that this second type of experience is more often a factor in the development of major depression.

We can then define depression as an intense and long-lasting painful experience which cannot be shared within the interpersonal field of an individual. Below we examine most prevalent interpersonal constellations that underlie depressive syndromes.

The Typical Quality of Interpersonal Configurations in Depressive Conditions

At the root of depressive phenomena there generally lies some interpersonal event or configuration. Pain can stem from events which endanger or hinder the satisfaction of basic needs, including attachment and wishes for care, narcissistic strivings, classical oedipal wishes, etc. However, when the frustration of basic needs is due to events that lie outside the reach of human power (death, illness, social or natural catastrophy), the medical paradigm is only rarely called into play. Some patients mention an unavoidable injury that was due to fate and identify it as the source of their depression, but these beliefs tend to function as defense mechanisms and tend to be aimed at concealing interpersonally relevant events.

The psycho-dynamically oriented clinical observation repeatedly shows that the symptoms of depression are generated by the frustration of basic human needs at the level of the subject's core interpersonal relationships. Their needs do not simply go unmet due to overwhelming impersonal, natural forces: depression strikes when a 'significant other' more or less intentionally and consistently fails to meet a subject's basic needs.

Bion's extended theory of projective identification may help us to understand how and why the active (albeit unconscious) introduction of negative feelings into a fellow human being can offer an individual an extremely valuable way to escape excessive suffering. Melanie Klein described projective identification as the process of "expelling dangerous substances (excrements) out of the self and into the mother." She went on to say: "Together with these harmful excrements, expelled in hatred, split-off parts of the ego are also projected on to the mother or, as I would rather call it, *into* the mother. These excrements and bad parts of the self are meant not only to injure but also to control and to take possession of the object. ... This leads to a particular form of identification which establishes the prototype of an aggressive object-relation. I suggest for these processes the term 'projective identification.' "[4] In Bion's words, "there exists an omnipotent phantasy that it is possible to split off temporarily undesired, though sometimes valued, parts of the personality and put them into an object." [5]

The subject who uses projective identification exploits a number of verbal and non-verbal behaviors with the aim of leading his current emotional partner to experience feelings which parallel his own. For instance, a mother who is tormented by feelings of jealousy towards her daughter-in-law may alienate a substantial proportion of the family real estate to this very woman, in order to stimulate intense feelings of jealousy in her own daughter. So, the mother's feelings come to be located within the arena of her daughter's awareness.

Whereas Melanie Klein described projective identification as a defense mechanism which was operative in severely disordered personalities under conditions of intense anxiety, Bion conceptualized it as a general principle of mental functioning, even the prototype form of mental activity, "an early form of that which later is called a capacity for thinking." [6] He pursued this line of thought further and considered projective identification as a basic mechanism in mother-child interaction and in relations characterized by parallel levels of intimacy and closeness, i.e. whenever there exists some container in which projected material can be received and then given back in a transformed state. [7]

Bion's extension of Melanie Klein's theory allows us to distinguish two basic projective configurations of exchange. At one pole, we find mostly aggressive interactions, where anxiety or pain-eliciting material is grossly evacuated into the object. At the other extreme, we encounter reciprocal exchanges of experiential material where distressing contents are processed by the object before they are handed back to the subject. If we examine typical depressive object relations in light of the extended theory of projective identification, we can observe that such growth oriented projective exchanges are exceedingly rare.

Core interpersonal relationships of depressed patients tend to be marked by aggression and frequently displays of sadomasochism. Typically, ß-elements, that is unarticulated violently negative emotions [8] are evacuated into the patient, and his capacity for digesting them or working them through becomes exhausted. His emotional stores are fully depleted.

From such a perspective, a number of phenomena which are traditionally described as symptoms of depression can be conceptualized as representations of emotional victimization experiences. In my clinical experience, these types of victimization experiences can be divided in two basic categories.

On the one hand, the main love object of some patients actually attacks them through blame, control, active withdrawal or reducing their core emotional resources, or by purposely giving to others what is particularly precious to the patient. In this first interpersonal configuration, the content of projective identification is distinctly aggressive, and projected β elements include aspects of unnamed desperation, pain, envy and jealousy.

In other clinical situations, the main form of pressure exerted by the patient's love object is the withdrawal of customary and needed love and care. The love-object is thus not overtly attacking the patient but rather keeping him in a state in which his needs and wishes are permanently unfulfilled. This leads to an escalation in his gratification seeking behaviors.

THE GENESIS OF DEPRESSIVE SYMPTOMS

Mental pain is an intra-psychic phenomenon. We may speculate on its cerebral or neuropsychological correlates, but must, for the time being, be content to study the phenomenological consequences on the patient's behavior and reflect on the reports he provides of his emotional life. In fact, it is reasonable to assume that *most or all clinical symptoms of depression are expressions of the impact of mental pain on several aspects of the patient's personality.*

In most cases, mental pain is explicitly included in a patient's report in terms of a feeling of sadness. However, in reality, the impact of mental pain on a patient's feelings and behaviors is much more extended and multifaceted. It affects a patient's everyday life experience through a number of distinct mechanisms: a) frustrating interpersonal interactions infiltrate the patient's fantasy life and find disguised *representation* in many symptoms of depression, b) the intensity of mental pain is apparently able to *hinder the optimal functioning of the mental apparatus*, and thereby conditions second group of symptoms of depression, c) mental pain actually contaminates and *inhibits many basic drives,* and finally d) the introjected aggression generated within the context of frustrating interpersonal interactions can elicit *interpersonal strategies* which underlie other manifest symptoms of depression.

We now review each of these pathogenetic pathways.

Symptoms as Representations of Painful Interpersonal Experiences

The depressed patient frequently feels his pain is partially or totally unmotivated, whereas the author assumes the contrary, namely, that intense mental pain has causes and that these causes are events in real life. Having just described the typical interpersonal configurations that may be associated with the development of such pain, we may summarize saying that the patients: a) have lost key figures or been displaced from roles that are necessary for their emotionally well-being; or b) have been violently attacked by one of the objects in their emotional environment; or c) be experiencing frustration in getting their basic needs met in the context of important interpersonal relationships.

These experiences do not constitute intra-psychic events but they are indeed *real* events that are taking place in *the patient's interpersonal life*. And, they are given representation in the patient's fantasy life. A number of the phenomena currently described as the symptoms of depression can in fact be conceptualized as representations of these emotional events.

Actual Losses.

The loss of elements vital to one's own interpersonal processes obviously takes place during mourning. But there is also the breaking up of core interpersonal relationships, through retirement, the departure of children or co-workers, or as a result of role changes associated with the life cycle. The latter can imply the definitive disappearance or death of important sources of emotional nourishment. And the death of important elements of personality or internal objects frequently surfaces in manifest fantasies and symptoms of depressed patients: they either feel dead, fear death or seek it. They thus depict a personality that is painfully lacking something essential.

Aggression on the Part of the Object

A second core class of experiences involved in the genesis of depression-related clinically observable phenomena comprises those items noted above: aggressive projective identification exchanges between the patient and the external objects in his interpersonal milieu. When the patient's love object pours hatred, attitudes of devaluation and sadism into his mind, the patient is invaded by feelings of hopelessness and despair. At the same time, his mental apparatus tends to be overburdened with emotion and information processing requirements which are clearly beyond the scope of its resources.

The resulting clinical phenomena can then be conceptualized either as representations of these emotional events or as direct consequences of the resources of the patient's mental apparatus having been inundated with negative information. The refusal to eat or the lack of interesting therein is a most direct representation of a love relation (the relationship to the breast in Kleinian terminology) in which the only emotional nourishment that is available has a distinctive noxious (or toxic, see Eigen, 1999) quality. We have already dealt with these phenomena in Ch. 4 (*see* p. 69).

A decline in interest in pleasurable activities certainly also implies that there are parallel issues. In terms of behavior, it represents the inability to take in or receive positive emotional stimuli from the environment. The patient being attacked by the object from whom he expects nurturance, refuses food, both actually and symbolically.

Loss of appetite represents interactional phenomena at a very basic level: it displays the essential character of a relationship, even if it conceals specific contents which the projective strategies of the object takes on in order to reach its goal. The low self-esteem so frequently observed in depressed patients or guilt feelings which have similar root causes attest to the specific ways this aggression may follow. The patient communicates that the libidinal investment from the object has dramatically been reduced.

Such a shift may, of course, be independent of the object's will. He may be emotionally incapacitated and so unable to invest the patient with narcissistic cathexis for a host of reasons, including real events in his current life such as illness, or mourning. Whatever the causes may be, both clinical experience with patients and evidence obtained from empirical research, point to the conclusion that the depressed subject is often the focus of particularly harsh criticism and blame from his intimate relations.

Freud initially deemed such criticism justified in terms of its content, but he considered it to be directed to an improper object. The depressed person's self-criticism should actually apply to the external or introjected love object.[9] However, in a subsequent paper he stated that guilt feelings and the generally negative self-image of depressed patients could be traced back to the particularly severe nature of the introjects of parental figures. These he took to constitute the basis of a subject's Super Ego.[10]

We must here content ourselves with the observation that the forms of blame which a depressed patient directs toward himself bears a striking resemblance to those received by his intimates in the *hic et nunc*. Apparently these form of blame serve the purpose of freeing the love-object from feelings of sadness, humiliation and desperation in so far as they are actively forced into the patient.

Inadequate Satisfaction of Needs

Even in adulthood, emotional well-being is crucially dependent on the availability of sources of need gratification in the interpersonal field. A caring wife or a dependable mother, a functioning psychoanalyst, or emotionally available humans in different social or familial roles can be the essential perquisite for the healthy emotional functioning of many, if not all, of us. The abrupt reduction or suppression of such nurturance functions compromises existing adjustments and is therefore the source of intense pain. Basic wishes and needs are no longer met.

The most immediate evidence of a low level of gratification of such basic needs is represented by an increase in wish-fulfilling activities. An increase in eating-related drives or behaviours or in the general level of psychomotor activity may be due in part to analogous phenomena, phenomena which have been interpreted as *ex-vacuo* activities from an ethological perspective (Lorenz, 1970).

According to Klein's analysis of manic-depressive illness (1935), an increase in the level of activity as well as in the intensity of drives reflects the fact that manic defense mechanisms have been activated. These manic defenses [11] aim at concealing the reality of loss and reassuring the self that some form of pain relief can be obtained without direct interaction with the love object.

Impairment of the Activity of the Mental Apparatus

The depressed patient represents the content and the quality of his core relationship through the symptoms listed above. But the actual transfer or exchange of quantities and qualities of emotions between the patient and his love objects cannot be lacking in evident consequences for the proper functioning of the patient's mental apparatus. The following metaphors may therefore be helpful: a) that of an overburdened truck: it can move only slowly and with extreme effort; and b) that of a room or space filled in with unhealthy gas: people staying within it are drowsy or somnolent. Their cognitive processes slowed down.

The mind of a patient who has received a large amount of negative or painful emotion is overburdened: initiating mental, and, consequently, somatic, movement is slow and persistent movement is painful. The clinical phenomenon of psychomotor retardation and asthenia thus appears. Drive-based activities are reduced in number and intensity. The fact that they are excessively laden of toxic or harmful gas-like contents overtaxes the patient's cognitive resources. Problem solving is hampered and sleepiness sets in.

This constellation may be associated with the clinical phenomena of hypersomnia, but when the overflow of unpleasant mental contents is particularly high, a peculiar phenomenon ensues. Sleep is generally possible only when the level of psychic and motor activity is reduced to a minimum. Human beings know too well that the level of stimuli from the environment must be kept to a minimum if sleep is to be established or maintained. We turn off the lights, shelter ourselves from noise, and blame the neighbors if they persist in making noise at late hours.

But, as was well known to the anchorites,[12] sleep can also result from overburdening the mental apparatus. This may be a sign that the mind cannot take on anything else. When too many negatively charged β-elements are introduced into the subject's mind, wakefulness is no longer possible. Mental activity is so slowed that sleep will ensue. However, this basically unnatural kind of sleep can last only as long as the mental apparatus is suppressed and filled with noxious emotional gas. As soon as the emotional vapors become dispersed and clear some mental pathways in the sufferer's brain (not currently describable in any detail), inhibitory mechanisms are relaxed. The intense and totally unprocessed emotional experiences of the previous day creep up on him, the mental apparatus once again gets moving, and sleep cannot continue.

A particular kind of sleep is that so ended, namely that which is due to the fact that mental pain overwhelms the patient's mental resources, and complete relaxation cannot be achieved. After this awaking, it is clearly not immediately possible to sleep again: the mental apparatus is now processing a huge body of information, and so is heavily engaged. The phenomenon which psychiatrists call 'terminal insomnia' has set in.

Mental Pain Infiltration of the Motivational Processes and Bodily Rhythms

When the motivational forces within the personality orient themselves towards rewarding activities, mental pain exerts a distinct inhibitory effect on them. Whether the search for gratification is carried out within the field of bodily based instincts (for nutrition, sexual satisfaction, parent-child contact or others), or in the context of the more symbolic or narcissistic gratifications offered by money, power, professional or intellectual achievements and so on, the depressed subject meets pain at the core of any and all of his efforts.

On the other hand, when the object of wish or need is actually acquired, it is often not satisfying as he had hoped. The negative quality of repressed pain often contaminates sexual pleasure as well as money, food and friendship. The interest in these aims thus decreases, a fact which is unhappily noted in the patients' relations and by observing clinicians.

Aggression on the part of a love object may disturb the fantasies of gratification associated with a patient's wish fulfillment-oriented activities; the burden of emotional pressure the subject has been subject to may come to inhibit motivation; but pain can affect pleasurable activities also through a third pathway, namely, by activating defense mechanisms.

Physical pain causes one to engage in activities through which it can be gotten rid of, e.g. fight or flight responses (Cannon, 1915). Similarly for mental pain, it stimulates activities aimed at freeing the personality of it. These activities can obviously be conceptualized in terms of the psychoanalytic theory of defense mechanisms. A number of these defenses, including repression and negation, modify the awareness of numerous mental contents, among them, pain. But pain cannot be put aside so easily. It inevitably resurfaces.

So, when the focus of perceptual activity is shifted from the interior locus of pain towards the physical body or external objects, the perceptual field tends to be more or less contaminated by this emotion, albeit *dissociated* from its cognitive content. The action that is necessary to obtain concrete or symbolic satisfaction begins to appear extremely labor intensive. For instance, our legs appear to ache when our brain signals to them to begin movement. In addition, the fact that mental activity is engulfed in emotional information is a distinct source of the psychomotor retardation, asthenia, and fatigue, one that is clinically observable in the depressed patient.

Introjected Aggression

Thusfar we have considered the extent to which emotional events in the patient's interpersonal field generate pain, and sought to determine how both emotional events and pain find representation as symptoms or stimulate those intrapsychic events which are the sources of the symptoms of depression. However, the clinical picture of depression cannot be thoroughly appreciated without the acknowledgement of the characteristic pathways along which pain proceeds in the human mind.

As noted, in animals, pain can evoke fight responses[13]. Their adaptive function is obvious. In fact, pain may also be due to the aggression by a predator or a competitor. Animal rage provide the emotional fuel for a counterattack on a possible aggressor. We do not know whether this aggressive response has been empirically documented in humans, but the observation of any fight between children or adults easily confirms the fact that this function is indeed extended to humans.

It is therefore no wonder that psychoanalytically oriented theorists have repeatedly observed an enhanced level of aggression in depressed patients' clinical material and interpersonal stances (*cfr.* above, pp. 91-92). As early as 1912, Karl Abraham traced the origin of depressive psychosis to "einer das Liebesvermögen paralysierenden Haßeinstellung" ("a hateful attitude which paralyzes the capacity for love." [14] And, in the more comprehensive theory of 1916, he identified one stage in drive development, which was distinctively dominated by aggressive oral wishes. A regression to this libidinal stage was a core feature of his theory of the psychogenesis of depressive states: "Vertiefte Einblicke in der Struktur der depressiven Psychosen haben mich zu der Annahme geführt, daß bei den Kranken *die Libido auf das primitivste uns bekannte Stadium ihrer Entwicklung regrediere*, auf jenes Stadium, welches wir als das orale oder kannibalistische bezeichnen lernten." [15] The existence of hateful and sadistic tendencies in depressive patients was acknowledged by the father of psychoanalysis, too, in his *Trauer und Melancholie.* [16]

Aggression can have different objects. It is not common in depressive disorders that it is expressed towards either enemies or associates. In depression, blame and even acted out, sometimes lethal aggression, is focused on the self. Freud interpreted the phenomenon in terms of the patient's identification with a disappointing love-object.[17] Depressive aggression would then be directed towards an introjected love-object.

However, on Freud's conceptualization of depression, aggression could in the end have as its target the disappointing love-object:

> ...pflegt es den Kranken noch zu gelingen, auf dem Umwege über die Selbstbestrafung Rache an den ursprünglichen Objekten zu nehmen und ihre Lieben

durch Vermittlung der Kranseins zu quälen, nachdem sie sich in die Krankheit begeben haben, um ihnen ihre Feindseligkeit nicht direkt zeigen zu müssen.[18]

...sick people are usually able, through the indirect way of self-punishment, to take their revenge on the originary objects and to torment their relatives through the instrument of their illness and for that they have taken refuge in the illness, not to be compelled to directly express their hostility towards them.

Aggression in depressed patients characteristically plays itself out in an indirect manner. Within the interpersonal field, it appears oriented towards the self. But, as Freud indicated, it also negatively affects the real objects who live in close contact with the patient.

Due to his inability to share responsibility of resource collection and the handling of family tasks, the patient is *de facto* enhancing the burden his or her partner has to bear. In so far as he withdraws from activity aimed at producing narcissistic or bodily pleasure, he is *de facto* reducing the amount of gratification his love-objects are getting from life.

Aggression is therefore a relevant motivational force underlying many manifest symptoms of depression: indeed, aggression is deemed a significant component within the mental processes which lead to the most tragic expression of mental suffering, namely, the taking of one's life. Acts of suicide have obvious negative consequences for the self, but in the patient's fantasy they are as much a way of causing severe injury to the objects' feelings of love and attachment towards the patient.

NOTES

1. Freud, 1917, pp. 430-431.
2. Paykel et al,. 1969; see also Shrout et al., 1989.
3. Gillespie, 1929; cfr. Jackson 1986, p. 211-212.
4. Klein, 1946, p. 8.
5. Bion, 1962, p. 31.
6. Ibidem, p. 37.
7. Ibidem, p. 89-94.
8. Bion, 1962, pp. 6-7.
9. Freud, 1917, pp. 431-435.
10. Freud, 1923, pp. 280-283.
11. Klein, 1935, p. 277-29
12. Evagrius, *De Octo spiritibus malitiae*, col. 1159B.
13. Zillman, 1979, pp. 81-82.
14. Abraham, 1912, p. 151.
15. Abraham, 1916, p. 108: "A thorough investigation into the structure of depressive psychoses led me to suppose that in affected *individuals libido regresses to the most*

primitive stage of its development which is known to us, to that stage which we have learned to know as oral or cannibalistic."

16. Freud, 1917, p. 438.
17. Ibidem, p. 439. Freud stated that "Die unzweifelhaft genußreiche Selbstquälerei bedeutet ganz wie das entschprechende Phänomen der Zwangsneurose die Befriedigung von sadistischen und Haßtendenzen. ..." ("The unquestionably pleasurable self-tormenting of melancholic states means, just as the corresponding phenomenon of the obsessive neurosis, the satisfaction of sadistic and hateful drives.")
18. Ibidem, p. 438.

Chapter Seven
Epistemological Observations

In Part III of the present book, we have suggested a model for the analysis of the process of the formation of depressive symptoms. In fig. 7.1, we summarized this by showing the emotional or object relation configurations underlying each symptom listed in DSM-IV diagnostic criteria for a Major Depressive Episode.

We were therefore able to develop a model for several psychological processes leading to clinical depression. From a purely theoretical point of view, we did not need to assume the existence of any dysfunction in the patient's mental apparatus to account for the symptoms. The proposed model is sufficient to explain all of the clinically observable phenomena identified as symptoms of depression in terms of the physiological functions of a human mind under unfavorable circumstances.

The model shows how people who are involved in negative interpersonal relationships or undergoing other negative life events may experience intense mental pain. This *emotional experience*, the experience of pain, though distressing, puzzling or embarrassing with reference to the patient's socially acceptable self-image, is *effectively* and *correctly* perceived by the patient.

In 1917, Freud proposed that some symptoms of melancholia could be traced back to the "direkt toxische Verarmung an Ichlibido."[1] The further development of psychoanalytically oriented psychiatry and the reflections presented here show that, at present, this restrictive assumption is not a *necessary* one. Psychologically meaningful mechanisms, which have individually been observed in operation in a number of clinical conditions, can lead from negative interpersonal events to pain, and from pain to experiences which are viewed as symptoms on current psychiatric theory.

Karl Popper (1935) claims that the main feature a scientific theory or proposition is expected to possess is its potential for falsification. Scientific knowledge differs from metaphysical postulates to the extent that the procedure for testing and refuting it can be specified. This condition of falsifiability should

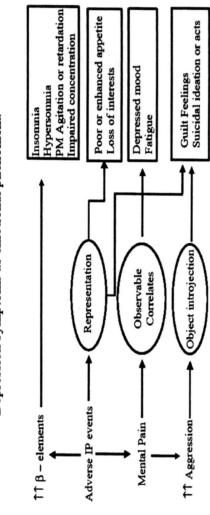

Fig. 7.1 – Flowchart representing the cuasative pathways leading from basic interpersonal and intrapsichic events to observable symptoms in depression. PM: Psychomotor; IP: Interpersonal

not be misinterpreted as a claim about the immediate and concrete availability of instruments suited for implementing the empirical testing of propositions. History teaches us that many scientific theories have been formulated several centuries before technological progress made it concretely possible to submit them to empirical testing. The conditions for falsifiability must rather be understood as referring to the possibility that empirical experiences relevant to assessing the applicability of a given proposition to reality can ever be constructed.

Can the model we have proposed here be conceptualized as a network of scientific statements from the point of view of Popper's epistemology? Or, does it represent a linguistic reformulation of the symptomatic phenomena of the depressive illness?

Our model enabled us to move from the level of discrete behaviors to that of interpersonal events or intra-psychic strategies. The descriptive approach of DSM nosography is targeted at those behaviors, (e.g. reports of sadness or happiness, eating or not eating) commonly observed in depressed patients. However, most of these behaviors are rooted in emotional events and drives and these can be inferred from, or are directly reported by, the patient (e.g. "I don't feel hungry," or "I feel sad," or "I would rather be dead").

The present model goes still further and links observed behaviors to the patient's interpersonal life. As illustrated earlier, it is possible to trace each of the symptoms of depression back to a number of changes in the patient's interpersonal field. These events heavily affect the emotional life. They are a source of specific changes in the emotional life of the patient, chiefly a source of mental pain.

It does not seem to me that this formulation can be thought of as a simple deepening or analysis of data embedded already in the terms describing the overt symptomatology of depression. The fields of interpersonal relations and inherent emotions are not covered by in the diagnostic criteria for depression. These criteria are rather concerned with events which happen in time and with people other than those who, in our formulation, are actually relevant to the production of mental pain and the consequent development of depression.

Most commonly, the events which we have described as the sources of the depressed patient's distress are massively denied by him, either as concerns their impact on their emotional life, or on their existence. Typically, they are ignored in clinical descriptions of depressed patients. So, this model includes new data, data not included in behavior-oriented clinical descriptions.

We must now face the question of whether these new data and their ties to clinical symptoms are empirically verifiable. To do this, we must first underscore the fact that all events underlying clinical depression in our model a) take place in the interpersonal field or b) are emotional consequences of the former. The events of class a) are, in principle, fully observable. Most of those which give rise to depression are, in my experience, changes in the configuration of the family, generally due to progression through the life-cycle: marriage, separation, loss of power in the relations to the younger generation, loss of nurturing functions from significant others, bereavement. These can potentially be catalogued, registered and measured. We can imagine conducting empirical observations of them and studying their prevalence within depressed patients as opposed to in the general population.

Empirical literature on life events and depression is indeed abundant and repeatedly shows that negative life events are associated with its development. However, clinical observation makes possible a much more subtle perception of the painful meaning of a given event. The clinician, in so far as he maps each patient's life event within his interpersonal framework, is able to grasp the immediate impact that such events can have on the patient's emotional and narcissistic needs. In particular, he can understand whether a concrete event (for instance loss of a job) affects the love and power relationship of the patient within his immediate entourage, if a young man or woman moving out of a family house amounts to emotionally detaching from the parents, if the marriage of a daughter displaces a housewife from her narcissistically invested role of the leading female figure in a household.

We can hope that researchers will be able to develop more specific empirical instruments for studying these hypotheses in the future. At very least, at this point, we can, I believe, state that item a) above, i.e. the claim that there is a link between depression and emotionally negative interpersonal events, is potentially empirically testable.

The second step in developing our model involves tracking the emotional consequences of painful events, following their impact from their initial occurrence in the external world to the development of a number of manifest behaviors, affects, and ideational dispositions, i.e. to symptoms. The main assumption of this component of our theory is that, generally speaking, symptoms of depression can be conceptualized as either representations of emotionally negative events or as psychological consequences of such events.

The clinician is in a position to directly observe such connections between events and symptoms. He can, for instance, listen to the criticisms angrily formulated by a patient's wife, and, in the same interview, also listen to the patient's parallel attitude of self-blame. He can also explore the interpersonal processes the patient is reporting and make the connection between them and the patient's difficulties in sleeping or finding solutions to his life problems.

Empirically documenting these etiological correspondences is however highly problematic. For the present, at least, rating scales which might be designed to detect such subtle interpersonal interactions do not exist.

Over the last few decades, research into the process of psychotherapy has developed a number of instruments for quantitatively assessing interpersonal relationships by tracking moment to moment interactions. Outstanding among them is the Structural Analysis of Social Behavior (SASB, Benjamin, 1974) system.

The SASB is an empirical method which enables the researchers to assess sequences of patient-therapist or patient to patient interactions during psychotherapy sessions (Alpher, 1991). However, this categorical system is very limited with respect to the clinicians' rich conceptualizations.

A still more fundamental difficulty arises in attempting to submit depression-generating mechanisms to empirical study. This is the system of defenses that prevail in these patients. One defense mechanism that is deployed with particular frequency is denial.

Denial is a mechanism through which "Ein verdrängter Vorstellungs- oder Gedankeninhalt kann also zum Bewußtsein durchdringen, unter der Bedingung, daß er sich verneinen läßt." [2]

It was first described by Freud and was subsequently considered by Melanie Klein to be a typical mode of defense in manic-depressive states.[3] In my experience it is very prevalent in both monopolar and bipolar depression.

The basic energy fueling denial is narcissism. In mood disorders, it protects the individual against the shocking awareness of the true, and sometimes frustrating, character of some of the interactions he or she is involved in.

In Ch. 4 of this book (*see* pp. 82-83), we mentioned that depressive patients are particularly afraid of acknowledging the aggression carried out against them, and the unsatisfactory amount of love they are getting from their main love-objects. To realize that they are not as important to their caregivers or lovers as they would hope is a clearly unbearable cognition.

It is for this reason that a patient's direct report is definitely an unreliable source of knowledge about depression and its mechanisms. Only the direct observation of significant interactions within both the therapeutic setting and the patient's ecological interpersonal field could truly shed empirical light on the mechanisms which underlie depression.

These reflections obviously indicate that there exists a number of pragmatic difficulties in empirically testing the model of the pathogenesis of depression proposed here. None of them, however, is a feature of the nature of the theory *per se*. At present, at least, technological limitations make it impossible to either test or refute the theory. But, it is rooted in (potentially) testable real events which occur in the interpersonal world. Some of them can be observed easily, others require instruments or research conditions which are not available as yet. Substantial progress is needed where methods and instruments for psychological research are concerned, but I believe that the theory as a whole can be considered scientific.

A second key question also surfaces here: If it is still lacking empirical validation, is the theory of any real value? In so far as its empirical basis is outside the scope of immediate investigation, can it make any contribution to current practice?

Many theories co-exist concurrently nowadays within the field of psychiatry and psychotherapy. And, many of them attempt to offer explanations of depressive syndromes, among them, models underlying cognitive therapy, psychoanalytic theory, interpersonal theory, and the monoaminergic theory of depression. Many of these theories acknowledge that they can answer only a number of questions about depression, master only a number of issues, while others may be better understood within different theoretical frameworks.

While all such theories can currently claim to possess some evidence of validity, none of them is presently in a position to offer a thorough and systematic empirical evidence of correspondence of its claims to clinical reality.

The many currently available theories of depression have a massive impact in the practice of psychiatry. They obviously guide research, but are, at the same time, frequently used by clinicians as a framework for formulating cases of depression. Each clinician's conceptualization of depression has a perceivable impact on the way he observes patients, gathers and systematizes clinically relevant information, sets therapy goals, plans and implements treatments, and understands their successes and failures.

From this pragmatic point of view, the value of a theory can be appreciated in terms of its ability to improve the clinical practice of mental health professionals adopting it. This is also obviously the case with the model we are presenting here. While we cannot currently state that it is a true representation of reality, we can try it out and assess its impact on practice.

Moreover, the adoption of a theory is not a merely mechanical process. It requires a significant correspondence between the basic assumptions underlying the model and basic professional identifications and therapeutic goals of the men and women who will be relying on it. And, these processes are affected by each professional's self-representation, within their personal and social fields.

If any of the readers of this work should note that the model of depression presented here parallels in some way his or her interests and experiences, we suggest trying to use it in formulating cases. It will soon become clear that its main hypothesis, namely, that depressive symptoms are representations of actual, painful emotional events, can have a powerful impact on practice.

As noted, we are often not in a position, especially after few clinical interviews, to grasp a patient's vital needs and understand how he or she proceeds in order to secure adequate satisfaction of them. Denial mechanisms play a prominent role in concealing these vital interests of the self from the eyes of strangers. However, operating on the hypothesis that the patient who is complaining of depression is experiencing a major upheaval in his emotional or interpersonal resources enhances the likelihood that the clinician can maintain a degree of empathy with the patient. Tracing out the mental processes and emotional events underlying the patient's symptoms actually helps the clinician to listen to the intense cry for help that he or she is sending out.

In fact, changes in the severity of symptoms can occur abruptly in the context of depressive syndromes, and we are less likely to be able to predict them if our knowledge of the patient's life and relations is limited. By contrast to this, whenever the clinician comes to some understanding of the current difficulties in a patient's emotional life, his conceptualization of that patient's depression is considerably deepened. The patient is no longer operating under the action of mysterious and unpredictable forces. Instead, the worsening or improvement of symptoms can now be tracked in parallel with emotional history. Any change in his intimate relationships is doomed to manifest itself sooner or later in changes in his clinical condition. Loss of interpersonal or family roles, power struggles, inward or outward flows of aggression and mental pain can be observed as can the consequences they have for the patient's mental processes and related symptoms.

If the therapeutic relation lasts, and if the patient and his intimates allow us a deeper contact with him and them, gradually a network of needs and goals begins to take shape. We begin to be aware of the situations which are likely to be experienced as harmful by the patient. Exacerbations of his suffering and of his depressive symptoms tend to then become less puzzling for the clinician.

This does not always lead to effective interventions. It is sometimes clear that the patient's well being would be improved, if we were to lend him some of the mental resources we have at our disposal. We might otherwise understand that the patient can benefit from the establishment of an intense relation with ourselves, from an understanding of the negative consequences of a maladaptive interpersonal pattern of his, from protection provided by the staff of a psychiatric ward, or from clinical work which involves his family or spouse. In such circumstances the principle of dynamic, interpersonal, cognitive psychotherapy, family therapy or dynamically oriented psychiatry can help in identifying and implementing such short- or long-term interventions.

Unfortunately, in many cases, the patient's interpersonal difficulties are long lasting and lie outside the reach of a therapeutic relation, or severe characteriological problems exist and do not allow him to choose less frustrating behaviors. But in my experience, working with a conceptualization of depression as involving both the effects of mental pain and the devices used to communicate them, may also make the task of the practicing psychiatry less frustrating and more tolerable. It is my hope that some of the readers of this work will be able to share this experience in their professional lives.

NOTES

1. "direct toxic weakening of libido," p. 446.
2. Freud, 1925, p. 12. "A repressed representation or thought content can reach the awareness, on the condition that it lets itself be denied."
3. Klein, 1935, pp. 277-278.

REFERENCES

Works first published in manuscript form are listed by the author's name and text title; those first published in printed form are listed by the author's name and date of publication. Quotations from the New Testament are taken from:

NESTLE-ALAND *Novun testamentum Graece*, 27. Auflage. Post Eberhard et Erwin Nestle communiter ediderunt Barbara et Kurt Aland, Johannes Karavidopoulos, Carlo M. Martini, Bruce M. Metzger. Deutsche Bibelgeschaft, Stuttgart, 1993

New Testament abbreviations comply with Abbreviation Style of *Catechismus Catholicae Ecclesiae*

Abraham K. (1912) Ansätze zur psychoanalytischen Erforschung und Behandlung des manisch-depressiven Irreseins und verwandter Zustände. *Zentralblatt für Psychoanalyse.* II(6), pp. 302-315. Also in (1999) *Psychoanalytische Studien*, ed. by J. Cremerius, Band II, pp. 146-162, Psychosozial-Verlag, Gießen.
———. (1916) Untersuchungen über die früheste prägenitale Entwicklungsstufe der Libido. *Internationale Zeitschrift für (ärztliche) Psychoanalyse*, IV(2), 71-97. Also in (1999) *Psychoanalytische Studien*, ed. by J. Cremerius, Band I, pp. 84-112, Psychosozial-Verlag, Gießen.
———. (1924) Versuch einer Entwicklungsgeschichte der Libido auf Grund der Psychoanalyse der seelischer Störungen. *Neue Arbeiten zur ärztlichen Psychoanalyse*, Heft 11, pp. 1-96. Also in (1999) *Psychoanalytische Studien*, ed. by J. Cremerius, Band I, pp. 113-183, Psychosozial-Verlag, Gießen.
Akiskal, H.P. (1995) Mood disorders: Clinical features. In. H.I. Kaplan & B.J. Sadock (Eds.), *Comprehensive Textbook of Psychiatry/VI*, Williams and Wilkins, Baltimore (pp. 1123-1152).
Alper V.S. (1991) Interdependence and parallel processes: A case study of structural analysis of social behavior in supervision and short-term dynamic psychotherapy. *Psychotherapy: Theory, Research, Practice, Training.* 28 (2) pp. 218-231.
American Psychiatric Association (1980), *Diagnostic and Statistical Manual of Mental Disorders. Third Edition. DSM-III,* American Psychiatric Association, Washington, DC.
———. (1987), *Diagnostic and Statistical Manual of Mental Disorders. Third Edition, Revised. DSM-III-R,* American Psychiatric Association, Washington, DC.
———. (1994), *Diagnostic and Statistical Manual of Mental Disorders. Fourth Edition. DSM-IV,* American Psychiatric Association, Washington, DC.

————. (2000a), *Diagnostic and Statistical Manual of Mental Disorders. Fourth Edition. Text Revision. DSM-IV-TR,* American Psychiatric Association, Washington, DC.

————. (2000b), *Practice Guidelines for the Treatment of Patients with Major Depressive Disorder,* American Psychiatric Association, Washington, DC.

Angst J. (1984) Switch from depression to mania: A record study over decades between 1920-1982. *Psychopathology,* 18: 140-154.

Arieti S. (1977) Psychotherapy of severe depression. *American Journal of Psychiatry.* 134: 864-868.

Aristoteles, *Problemata Physica.* Ed. by H. Knoellinger, J. Klek & Ch. E. Ruelle (1922) Aristoteles, *Problemata Physica,* Teubner, Leipzig.

Augustinus, Aurelius, *Confessionum libri XIII.* Mod. ed. by M. Simonetti, with a transl. by G. Chiarini (1992) *Sant'Agostino. Confessioni.* 5 voll. Fondazione Lorenzo Valla-Arnoldo Mondadori Editore, Verona.

Azzone P. (2001) Incontrare la depressione nei servizi di salute mentale: il contributo della letteratura psicoanalitica. *Rivista di Psichiatria,* 36, pp. 313-322.

————. (2008) Melancolia e accidia: dolore scientifico e dolore religioso. In Viganò C., Azzone P., Morandi C. (a cura di) *La mente dell'anima: Incontri al confine tra esperienza del sacro e psicoanalisi.* Aracne editrice, Roma, pp. 155-170.

Beck A.T., Rush A.J., Shaw B.F., Emery G. (1979) *Cognitive Therapy of Depression.* The Guilford Press, New York.

Beck A.T. & Weishaar M. (1989) Cognitive therapy. In A. Freeman, K.M. Simon, L.E. Beutler, H. Arkowitz (Eds.) *Comprehensive Handbook of Cognitive Therapy* (pp. 21-36). Plenum Press, New York.

Benjamin L. (1974) Structural analysis of social behavior. *Psychological Review.* 81, pp. 392-425.

Bergeret J. (1976) Dépressivité et dépression dans la cadre de l'économie défensive. *Revue Français de Psychanalyse,* 5-6: 1019.

Berrios G.E. (1995) Mood Disorders: Clinical section. In G.E. Berrios & R. Porter (Eds.) *A History of Clincal Psychiatry: The Origin and History of Psychiatric Disorders* (pp. 384-408). The Athlone Press, London & New Brunswick, NJ.

————. (1996) *The History of Mental Symptoms: Descriptive Psychopathology since the Nineteenth Century.* Cambridge University Press, Cambridge

Biancosino B., Bonatti L., Grassi L. (2000) Quando le lacrime sono parole: l'importanza dei modelli psicodinamici nella comprensione e nella cura della depressione. *Psichiatria e Psicoterapia Analitica,* 19: 208-217.

Bibring E. (1953) The mechanism of depression. In *Affective Disorders: Psychoanalytical Contributions to Their Study,* Ed. P. Greenacre. International Universities Press, New York, pp. 13-48.

Bion W.R. (1962) *Learning from Experience.* William Heinemann Medical Books, London.

————. (1975) *The dream.* Imago Editora Ltda., Rio de Janeiro. Republished in (1991) *A Memoir of the Future,* Karnac Books, London, pp. 1-217.

Böker H., Hell D., Budischewski K., Eppel A., Härtlig F., Rinnert H., von Schmelling F., Will H., Schoeneich F., Northoff G. (2000) Personality and object relations in patients with affective disorders: Idiographic research by means of the repertory grid technique. *Journal of Affective Disorders,* 60: 53-59.

Bonhöffer A.F. (1911) *Epictet und das Neue Testament,* Töpelmann, Gießen.

Bucknill J.Ch. & Tuke D.H. (1858) *A Manual of Psychological Medicine.* Blanchard and Lea, Philadelphia.

Burton R. (1628) *The Anatomy of Melancholy*, 3rd ed. Mod. ed. by H. Jackson e W.H. Gass (2001) The New York Review of Books, New York.

Cannon W.B. (1915) *Bodily Changes in Pain, Hunger, Fear and Rage: An Account of Recent Researches into the Function of Emotional Excitement*. Appleton and Co., New York and London.

Casagrande C. & Vecchio S. (2000) *I sette vizi capitali: Storia dei peccati nel medioevo*. Einaudi, Torino.

Cassianus, Joannes. *De Coenobiorum Institutis*. Ed. by J.-P. Migne in *Patrologiae Latinae cursus completus* Vol. 49, coll. 53-476. Trad. it. a cura di L. Dattrino (1989) Giovanni Cassiano. *Le istituzioni cenobitiche*. Abbazia di Praglia, Bresseo di Teolo (Padova).

Celsus, Aulus Cornelius, *De medicina*. Ed. e trad. it. a cura di Angiolo del Lungo (1904) Aulo Cornelio Celso, *Della medicina*. Sansoni Editore, Firenze.

Chaucer, Geoffrey, *The Canterbury Tales*. Ed. in Benson, L.D. (ed.) *The Riverside Chaucer*, pp. 3-328. Houghton Mifflin Company, Boston.

Colapietro, V. (1997) Acedia: A case study of a deadly sin and a lively sign. *Semiotica*, 117-2/4: 357-380.

Costantinus Africanus, *Libri duo de melancholia*. Ediz a cura di K. Garbers in (1993) Ishaq ibn Imran, *Maqala fi l-malihulia (Abhandlung über die Melancholie)* und Constantini Africani *Libri duo de melancholia*. Ariadne-Fachverlag, Aachen.

Crichton A. (1798) *An Inquiry into the Nature and Origin of Mental Derangement*. Cadell-Davis, London.

Cross-National Collaborative Group (1992) The changing rate of major depression: Cross-national comparisons. *Journal of the American Medical Association*, 268: 3098-3105.

Cujpers P., van Straten A., & Warmerdam L. (2007) Behavioral activation treatments of depression: a meta-analysis. *Clinical Psychology Review*, 27:318-326.

Dante Alighieri. *Commedia*. Edizione a cura di E. Pasquini e A. Quaglio (1987), Garzanti, Milano

Diogenes Laertius, *De Vitis et Dogmatibus Clarorum Philosophorum*, Ed. by R.D.Hicks (1925) Diogenes Laertius. *Lives of eminent philosophers*. Harvard University Press, Cambridge Ms.

Druss B.G., Hoff R.A., Rosenheck R.A. (2000) Underuse of anti-depressants in major depression: Prevalence and correlates in a national sample of young adults. *Journal of Clinical Psychiatry*, 61: 234-237.

Du Laurens A. (1597) *Discours de la conservation de la veuë: des maladies melancholiques: des catarrhes: & de la vieillesse. Reveuz de noveau & augmentez de plusieurs chapitres*. Iamet Mettayer, Paris.

Ehrenberg A. (1998) *La fatigue d'être soi. Dépression et societé*. Editions Odile Jacob, Paris; trans. (Italian) (1999) *La fatica di essere se stessi: Depressione e società*. Giulio Einaudi editore, Torino.

Eigen M. (1999) *Toxic Nourishment*. Karnac Books, London.

Elkin I. (1994) The NIMH Treatment of Depression Collaborative Research Program: Where we began and where we are. In A.E. Bergin & S.L. Garfield (Eds.) *Handbook of Psychotherapy and Behaviour Change*. John Wiley & Sons, New York, pp. 114-142.

Ellis A. (1962) *Reason and Emotion in Psychotherapy*. L. Stuart, New York.

Engel G.L. (1977) The need for a new medical model: a challenge for biomedicine. *Science*, 196: 129-136.

Engstrom E.J. (1995) Kreapelin: Social Section. In G.E. Berrios & R. Porter (Eds.) *A History of Clincal Psychiatry: The Origin and History of Psychiatric Disorders* (pp. 292-301). The Athlone Press, London & New Brunswick, NJ.

Epictetus. *Enchiridion*. W.A. Oldfather, Ed. and Trans (English) (1928) The Enchiridion of Epictetus. In *Epictetus*. Vol. II (pp. 482-537). Harvard University Press, Cambridge, MA..

Esquirol E. (1838) *Des maladies mentales considérées sous le rapports médical, hygiénique et medico-legal.* J.-B. Bailliére, Paris.

Evagrius Ponticus, *De Malignis Cogitationibus.*P. Gehin & C. Guillaumont, Eds., trans. (French) (1971) *Sur les pensées.* Sources Chrétiennes 438. Les Éditions du Cerf, Paris.

———. *De Octo Spiritibus Malitiae.* Ed. by J.- P. Migne, in *Patrologia Graeca* (Vol. 79, coll. 1145 A - 1164 D).

———. *Practicos.* A. Guillaumont & C. Guillaumont. Eds. & Trans (French) (1971) Évagre le Pontique. *Traité pratique ou le moine,* 2 Tomes. Sources Chrétiennes 170-171, Les Éditions du Cerf, Paris.

Fenichel O. (1945) trad. it. (1951) Depressione e Mania. In *Trattato di Psicoanalisi.* Astrolabio, Roma.

Ficino, Marsilio (1489) *De triplici vita* . Firenze. Ed. (1576) in *Opera Omnia*, Basel.

Fisher S., Greenberg R. (Eds.) (1997), *From Placebo to Panacea: Putting Psychiatric Drugs to Test.* John Wiley & Sons, New York.

Fornari F. (1981) *Il codice vivente. Femminilità e maternità nei sogni delle madri in gravidanza.* Boringhieri, Torino.

Foucault M. (1961) *Folie et déraison: Histoire de la folie à l'âge classique.* Plon, Paris.

Freud S. (1896) Weitere Bemerkungen über die Abwehr-Neuropsychosen. *Neurologisches Zentralblatt,* 10. Also in (1952) *Gesammelte Werke, I. Band.* Ed. E. Bibring, W. Hoffer, E. Kris, O. Isakower. Imago Publishing, London, pp. 377-403.

———. (1907) Die "kulturelle" sexualmoral und die moderne Nervosität. In *Grenzfragen des Nerven- und Seelenlebens,* LVI, Ed. v.L. Löwenfeld, Wiesbaden; Also in (1941) *Gesammelte Werke, VII. Band.* Ed. E. Bibring, W. Hoffer, E. Kris, O. Isakower. Imago Publishing, London, pp. 141-167.

———. (1910) *Eine Kindheits Erinnerung des Leonardo Da Vinci,* Deuticke, Leipzig und Wien (II ed. 1919, III ed. 1923); Also in (1943) *Gesammelte Werke, VIII. Band.* Ed. E. Bibring, W. Hoffer, E. Kris, O. Isakower. Imago Publishing, London, pp. 128-211.

———. (1914) Zur Einführung des Narzissmus. *Jahrbuch der Psychoanalyse,* 6:1-24.; Also in (1946) *Gesammelte Werke, X. Band.* Ed. E. Bibring, W. Hoffer, E. Kris, O. Isakower. Imago Publishing, London, pp. 137-170.

———. (1916-17) *Vorlesungen zur Einfürung in die Psychoanalyse.* 3 Voll., Oktav. Verlag Hugo Heller & Cie., Leipzig und Wien. Also in (1940) *Gesammelte Werke, XI. Band.* Ed. E. Bibring, W. Hoffer, E. Kris, O. Isakower. Imago Publishing, London.

———. (1917) Trauer und Melancholie. *Internationale Zeitschrift für Ärztliche Psychoanalyse,* 4, 288-301; Also in (1946) *Gesammelte Werke, X. Band.* Ed. E. Bibring, W. Hoffer, E. Kris, O. Isakower. Imago Publishing, London, pp. 427-446.

———. (1923) *Das Ich und das Es.* Internationale Psychoanalytischer Verlag, Leipzig-Wien- Zürich; Also in (1940) *Gesammelte Werke, XIII. Band.* Ed. E. Bibring, W. Hoffer, E. Kris, O. Isakower. Imago Publishing, London, pp. 237-289.

————. (1925) Die Verneinung. *Imago*, 11, pp. 217-221. Also in (1948) *Gesammelte Werke, XIV. Band.* Ed. E. Bibring, W. Hoffer, E. Kris, O. Isakower. Imago Publishing, London, pp. 9-15.

Gabbard G.O. (1990) *Psychodynamic Psychiatry in Clinical Practice.* American Psychiatric Press, Washington, DC. Trans. (Italian) (1992) *Psichiatria psicodinamica.* Raffaello Cortina Editore, Milano.

Galen, Claudius, *Ars Medica.* Ed. and Latin trans. by C.G. Kühn in (1821) *Claudii Galeni Opera Omnia,* Tomus I (pp. 305-412). Leipzig. Reprinted (1965) Georg Olms Verlagsbuchhandlung, Hildesheim.

————. *De Locis Affectis. Ed. and Latin trans. by* C.G. Kühn in (1824) *Claudii Galeni Opera Omnia.* Tomus VIII. (pp. 1-452), Leipzig. Reprinted (1965) Georg Olms Verlagsbuchhandlung, Hildesheim.

Gillespie R.D. (1929) The clinical differentiation of types of depression. *Guy's Hospital Reports,* 79: 306-344.

Gnoli R. (Ed.) (2001) *La rivelazione del Buddha. I testi antichi.* Arnoldo Mondadori Editore, Milano.

Gorad D.A., Gomborone J.E., Libby G.W., Farthing M.J.G. (1996) Intestinal transit in anxiety and depression. *Gut,* 39: 551-555.

Green A.I., Mooney J.J., Posener J.A. Schildkraut J.J. (1995) Mood disorders: Biochemical aspects. In H.I. Kaplan & B.J. Sadock (Eds.) *Comprehensive Textbook of Psychiatry/VI.* 6th edition, Vol. 1 (pp. 1089-1102). Williams & Wilkins, Baltimore.

Gregorius Magnus, *Moralia in Iob.* Edizione a cura di J.-P. Migne in *Patrologiae Latinae cursus completus* (Vol. 75, col. 509D - Vol. 76, col. 782A).

Griesenger W. (1845) *Die Pathologie und Therapie der Psychischen Krankheiten.* Krabbe, Stuttgart, 1845.

Grmek M.D. (1993) Il concetto di malattia. In M.D. Grmek (a cura di) *Storia del Pensiero medico occidentale: 1. Antichità e medioevo* (pp. 323-347). Editori Laterza, Roma-Bari.

Guillaume de Lorris, Jean de Meun, *Le roman de la rose.* Edizione a cura di A. Strubel (1992) Librairie Générale Française, Paris.

Guillaumont A. (1971). Étude historique et doctrinale. In Guillaumont A., Guillaumont C. (Eds.) *Évagre le Pontique. Traité pratique ou le moine,* Tomo I, pp. 21-125. Sources Chrétiennes 170, Les Éditions du Cerf, Paris.

Haynal A. (1977) Le sens du désespoir. *Revue Français de Psychanalyse,* 96.

Heimann P. (1950) On counter-transference. *Int. J. Psycho-Anal.* 31, pp. 81-84.

Hinshelwood R.D. (1993) *Clinical Klein.* Free Associations Books; tr. it. (1994) *Il modello Kleiniano nella clinica.* Raffello Cortina editore, Milano.

Hippocrates, *Aforismorum Libri.* Ed. and trans. (English) by W.H.S. Jones in (1931) *Hippocrates. Volume IV* (pp. 97-221). Harvard University Press, Cambridge, Ms.

————. *De Internis Affectionibus.* Ed. and French Transl. by É. Littré in (1851) Oeuvres Complètes d'Hippocrate. Tome 7me. J.B. Bailliere, Paris, pp. 166-303.

————. *Epidemiae III.* Edizione e traduzione inglese a cura di W.H.S. Jones in (1923) *Hippocrates. Volume I* (pp. 218-287). Harvard University Press, Cambridge, Ms.

————. *De Morbo Sacro.* Ed. Mod. e trad. it. (1983) In V. Di Benedetto & Lami A. (a cura di) *Ippocrate. Testi di medicina Greca.* (pp. 216-235). Rizzoli, Milano.

Honkalampi K., Hintikka J., Tanskanen A., Lehtonen J., Viinamäki H. (2000) Depression is strongly associate with alexithymia in the general population. *Journal of Psychosomatic Research,* 48: 99-104.

Ishaq ibn Imran, *Maqala fi l-malihulia (Manuale sulla Melancolia).* Edizione e trad. tedesca a cura di K. Garbers in (1993) Ishaq ibn Imran, *Maqala fi l-malihulia (Ab-*

handlung über die Melancholie) und Constantini Africani *Libri duo de melancholia.* Ariadne-Fach-Verlag, Aachen.

Jackson S.W. (1986) *Melancholia and Depression: From Hippocratic Times to Modern Times.* Yale University Press, New Haven - London.

Jaspers K. (1959) *Allgemeine Psychopathologie,* VII, Ed & Trans (Italian). (1964) *Psicopatologia generale.* Il Pensiero Scientifico Editore, Roma

Jindal R.D. & Thase M. E. (2003) Integrating psychotherapy and pharmacotherapy to improve outcomes among patients with mood disorders. *Psychiatric Services,* 54: 1484-1490.

Kant I. (1781-1787) *Kritik der Reinen Vernuft.* Mod. ed. of second edition in W. Dilthey (Ed.) (1911) *Kant's gesammelte Schriften.* Band 3. Georg Reimer, Berlin

Karasu T.B. (1990a) Toward a clinical model of psychotherapy for depression, I: Systematic comparison of three psychotherapies. *American Journal of Psychiatry,* 147: 133-147

———. (1990b) Toward a clinical model of psychotherapy for depression, II: An integrative and selective treatment approach. *American Journal of Psychiatry,* 147: 269-278

Kasper S., Gastpar M., Müller W.E., Volz H.P., Dienel A., Kieser M., Möller H.J. (2008) Efficacy of St. John's Wort extract WS 5570 in acute treatment of mild depression: a reanalysis of data from controlled clinical trials. *European Archives of Psychiatry & Clinical Neurosciences,* 258(1), pp. 59-63.

Keller M.B., Klerman G.L., Lavori P.W., Fawcett J.A., Coryell W., Endicott J. (1982) Treatment received by depressed patients. *Journal of the American Medical Association,* 248: 1848-1855.

Kernberg O.F. (1984) *Severe Personality Disorders.* Yale University Press, New Haven/ London. Trans (Italian). (1987) *Disturbi gravi della personalità.* Bollati Boringhieri editore, Torino.

Kernberrg O.F. (1988) Clinical dimensions of masochisms. In R.A. Glick e D.I. Meyers (a cura di) *Masochism: Current Psychoanalytic Perspectives* (pp. 61-79). Analytic Press, Hillsdale, NJ.

Klein M. (1935) A contribution to the psychogenesis of manic-depressive states. *International Journal of Psychoanalysis,* vol. 16; Also in (1975) *The Writings of Melanie Klein—Volume II: Love, guilt and reparation and Other Works 1921-1945.* The Free Press, New York, pp. 262-289.

———. (1946) Notes on some schizoid mechanisms. *International Journal of Psycho-Analysis,* 27. Also in (1975) *The Writings of Melanie Klein—Volume III:* Envy and Gratitude *and Other Works 1946-1963.* The Free Press, New York, pp. 1-24.

———. (1952) Some theoretical conclusions regarding the emotional life of the infant. In Klein M., Heimann P., Isaacs S. & Riviere J. (Eds.) *Developments in Psychoanalysis.* Hogarth Press, London. Also in (1975) *The Writings of Melanie Klein—Volume III:* Envy and Gratitude *and Other Works 1946-1963.* The Free Press, New York, pp. 61-93.

Kleinman A., & Good B. (1985) Introduction: Culture and depression. In A. Kleinman & B. Good (Eds.) *Culture and Depression: Studies in Anthropology and Cross-cultural Psychiatry of Affect and Disorder.* University of California Press, Berkley, pp. 1-33.

Klerman G.L., Weissman M.M. (1989) Increasing rates of depression. *Journal of the American Medical Association,* 15: 2229-2235.

Klerman G.L., Weissman M.M. Rousanville B.J., Chevron E.S. (1984) *Interpersonal Psychotherapy of Depression.* Basic Books, New York.

Klibansky R., Panofsky E., Saxl F. (1964) *Saturn and Melancholy: Studies in the History of Natural Philosophy, Religion, and Art.* Basic Books, New York. New improved German edition (1990) *Saturn und Melancholie.* Suhrkamp Verlag, Frankfurt am Main.

Kohut H. (1971) *The Analysis of the Self: A Systematic Approach to the Psychoanalytic Treatment of Narcissistic Personality Disorders.* International University Press, New York.

Kraepelin E. (1896) *Psychiatrie. Ein Lehrbuch für Studirende und Ärzte.* 5th ed., Johann Ambrosius Barth, Leipzig.

———. (1899) *Psychiatrie. Ein Lehrbuch für Studirende und Ärzte.* 6th ed. Johann Ambrosius Barth, Leipzig.

———. (1901) Tr. it. (1905) *Introduzione alla clinica psichiatrica: trenta lezioni.* Società editrice libraria, Milano.

———. (1902) *Clinical Psychiatry: A Textbook for Students and Physicians,* transl. and adapt. by A. Ross Defendorf from *Lehrbuch der Psychiatrie.* 7th Ed. MacMillan, New York.

Krafft-Ebing R. von (1879) *Lehrbuch der Psychiatrie.* Enke, Stuttgart.

Kramer P.D. (1993) *Listening to Prozac.* Penguin Books, London-New York.

Ladep N.G., Obindo T.J., Audu M.D., Okeke E.N., Malu A.O. (2006) Depression in patients with irritable bowel syndrome in Jos, Nigeria. *World Journal of Gastroenterology,* 12: 7844-7847.

Lax R. (1989) The narcissistic investment in pathological character traits and the narcissistic depression: Some implications for treatment. *International Journal of Psycho-Analysis,* 70: 81-90.

Le Goff J. (1960) Etudes au Moyen-Age: Temps de l'église et temps du marchand. *Annales. Economies sociétes, civilizations,* 3 , May-June.

Le Pape A., Lecomte T. (1996) *Aspects socioéconomiques de la dépression. Evolution 1980-1981/1991-1992.* CREDES.

Littré É. & Robin Ch. (eds.) (1855) *Dictionnaire de médicine, de chirurgie, de pharmacie, des sciences accessoires et de l'art vétérinaire de P.-H. Nysten, Dixième édition entièrement refondue par E. Littrè et Ch. Robin.* J.-B. Baillière, Paris.

Lopez D. e Zorzi L. (1990) *Dalla depressione al sorgere della persona.* Raffaello Cortina editore, Milano.

Lorenz K. (1970) The establishment of the instinct concept. In *Studies in Animal and Human Behaviours.* Harvard University Press, Cambridge.

Ludwig A.M. (1975) The psychiatrist as physician. JAMA 234: 603-604.

Maggiolini A. (1988) *La teoria dei codici affettivi di F. Fornari.* Edizioni Unicopli, Milano.

Mahler M. (1968) *On Human Symbiosis and the Vicissitudes of Individuation. Vol. 1: Infantile Psychosis.* International Universities Press, New York. Trans. (Italian) (1972) *Le psicosi infantili,* Boringhieri editore, Torino.

Meltzer D., Bremner J., Hoxter Sh., Weddell D., Wittenberg I. (1975) *Explorations in Autism: A Psycho-Analytical Study.* The Roland Harris Educational Trust, London. Tr. it. (1977) *Esplorazioni sull'autismo: Studio psicoanalitico.* Bollati Boringhieri editore, Torino.

Montgomery R.W. (1993) The ancient origins of cognitive therapy: The reemergence of stoicism. *Journal of Cognitive Psychotherapy,* 7: 5-19.

Moscovici S. (2001) *Social Representations: Explorations in Social Psychology.* New York University Press, New York.

Ogden Th. (1989) *The Primitive Edge of Experience*. Jason Aronson, London-Nortvale, N.J.

Paykel E., Myers J., Dienelt M., Klerman G., Lindenthal J., Pepper M. (1969), Life events and depression: A controlled study. *Archives of General Psychiatry*, 21:753-760.

Pflaster N.L. & Pedley T.A. (1996) A rational approach to the management of epilepsy. In S. Chokroverty (Ed.) *Management of Epilepsy* (pp. 25-45). Butterworth-Heinemann, Boston.

Phillips K.A., Gunderson J.G., Triebwasser J., Kimble C.R., Faedda G., Kyoon Lyoo I., Renn J. (1998) Reliability and validity of depressive personality disorder. *American Journal of Psychiatry*, 155: 1044-1048.

Piattoli R. (1950) *Codice diplomatico dantesco*. Gonnelli, Firenze.

Pinel, P. (1801) *Traité médico-philosphique sur l'aliénation mentale ou la manie*. Richard, Caille et Ravier Libraires, Paris

Pitcain A. (1718) *The philosophical and Mathematical Elements of Physick*. Andrew Bell and John Osborne, London,

Popper K.R. (1935) *Logik der Forschung*. Julius Springer Verlag, Wien.

Rather L.J. (1968) The "six things non natural": A note on the origins and fate of a doctrine and a phrase. *Clio Medica*, 3, 337-347.

Ribot Th. A. (1896), *La psychologie des sentiments*, Ancienne Librairie Germer Baillière et Cie Félix Alcan, Editeur, Paris. Eng. Ed. (1897) *The Psychology of emotions*, W. Scott, London.

Ries Merikangas K. & Kupfer D.J (1995) Mood disorders: Genetic aspects. In H.I. Kaplan & B.J. Sadock (Eds.) *Comprehensive Textbook of Psychiatry/VI*. 6th Ed. Vol. 1 (pp. 1102-1116). Williams & Wilkins, Baltimore.

Roth A. & Fonagy P. (1996) *What Works for Whom? A Critical Review of Psychotherapy Research*. The Guilford Press, New York.

Rousseau G. (2000) Depression's forgotten genealogy: notes towards a history of depression. *History of Psychiatry*, 11: 71-106.

Rufus Ephesius, *Fragmenta*. Edizione e trad. fr. a cura di Ch. Daremberg e Ch. É. Ruelle (1879) *Ouvres de Rufus d'Éphèse*. L'Impimerie Nationale, Paris.

Rush B. (1827) *Medical Inquiries and Observations upon the Diseases of the Mind*, 3rd Ed., J.Grigg, Philadelphia.

Schaffer S. (1988) Astronomers mark time: Discipline and the personal equation. *Science in Context*, 2, pp. 101-131.

Scott J. (2001) Cognitive therapy for depression. *British Medical Bulletin*, 57: 101-113.

Shrout P., Link B., Dohrenwend B., Skodol A., Stueve A., Mrotznik J. (1989) Characterizing life events as risk factors for depression: the role of fateful loss events. *Journal of Abnormal Psychology*, 95: 460-467.

Sickels E.M. (1932) *The Gloomy Egoist: Moods and Themes of Melancholy from Gray to Keats*. New York, Columbia University Press.

Spitzer R.L., Endicott J., Robins E. (1975) *Research Diagnostic Criteria (RDC)*. Biometrics Research, New York Psychiatric Institute, New York.

Stefanis C.N., Stefanis N.C. (1999) Diagnosis of depressive disorders: a review. In M. Maj & N. Sartorius (Eds.) *Depressive Disorders* (pp. 1-51). John Wiley & Sons, Chichester. Trans. (Italian) (2001) Diagnosi dei disturbi depressivi: una review. In *Disturbi depressivi* (pp. 1-47). CIC Edizioni Internazionali, Roma.

Szasz T.S. (1961) *The Myth of Mental Illness: Foundations of a Theory of Personal Conduct*. Hoeber-Harper, New York.

Thomas Aquinas, *Questiones disputatae de malo*. Edition by Frati minori in (1982) S. Thomae Aquinatis Doctoris Angelici, *Opera Omnia*, t. 23, Commissio Leonina, Vrin, Roma-Paris. Partial ed. [De vitiis capitalibus] and Trans. (Italian) U. Galeazzi (1996) Tommaso D'Aquino, *I vizi capitali*. RCS Rizzoli, Milano.

Tustin F. (1986) *Autistic Barriers in Neurotic Patients*. Karnac Books, London. Tr. it. (1990) *Barriere autistiche in pazienti nevrotici*. Borla, Roma.

Weber M. (1905) Die protestantische Ethik und der Geist des Kapitalismus. *Archiv für Sozialwissenschaft und Sozialpolitik*, 20 e 21. Tr. it. (1991) *L'etica protestante e lo spirito del capitalismo*. RCS Rizzoli Libri, Milano.

Willis Th. (1683) *Two Discourses Concerning the Souls of Brutes which is that of the Vital and Sensitive of Man*, trans. S. Pordage, Thomas Ring, Ch. Harper and John Leigh, London.

Winnicot D. (1953) Psychosis and child care. *British Journal of Medical Psychology*, 26. Tr. it. (1975) La psicosi e l'assistenza al bambino. In *Dalla pediatria alla psicoanalisi* (pp. 264-274). G. Martinelli, Firenze

Winnicott D.W. (1947) Hate in countertransference. *International Journal of Psycho-Analysis*, 30, p. 69ff; also in (1958) *Through Pediatrics to Psychoanalysis*. Tavistock Publications, London.

Xenakis I. (1969) *Epictetus: Philosopher-therapist*. Martinus Nijhoff, The Hague.